PREFACE

The United Kingdom of Great Britain and Northern Ireland, often called Britain in popular speech, consists of England, Wales, Scotland, and six counties in Northern Ireland. Its constitution is English in origin; and though it extends, of course, to the entire United Kingdom, it is frequently spoken of as the English constitution. The United Kingdom is exceptional in not possessing a written con▓▓▓▓▓▓ere is ▓othing in the British system of go▓▓▓▓▓▓alog▓▓ to the document known as the Consti▓▓▓▓e U▓▓ed States, and the absence of such a doc▓▓▓explain▓ important differences between the British▓▓▓▓e Amer▓can constitutional systems. But it does not i▓▓y the lack of a constitutional system, and it is of a constitutional system that we think when we speak of the British (or English) constitution. For our purposes, constitutional may be taken to mean governmental, a constitutional system to mean a governmental system, and constitutional rules to mean rules relating to government.

The British constitution has never been authoritatively defined; and the rules, indefinite in number, in which it is embodied are widely scattered. Many of them are rules of law—of statute law and of common law—legally binding and enforceable under decisions of law courts. Others are rules of usage and practice, commonly spoken of as conventions of the constitution, not legally binding or enforceable, though habitually observed. Thus the rule that taxes may be imposed only with the consent of parliament is a rule of statute law, to be found in the statute known as the Bill of Rights (1689); and the rule that the king or reigning queen, and nobody else, may summon and dissolve parliament is a rule of common law, for the power in question has never been conferred upon the monarch by statute or any form of enactment. Like all the other royal powers that constitute the royal prerogative it is derived from the common law, which is to be found in judicial opinions recorded in the reports of

8463

3

cases tried in the law courts. On the other hand, and in contrast with legal rules, the rule that meetings of the cabinet are summoned by the prime minister is a convention, not a law. So far as law (statute or common) is concerned, there need not be a cabinet or a prime minister.

It is essential to realize the great importance of conventions in the British constitutional system. They control the exercise of legal powers, especially the legal powers of the crown, and in some cases virtually nullify them. The more important of these conventions are the usages and understandings which enable the constitution to be operated in accordance with prevail   constitutional theory. A purely legalistic escri   resent British constitutional system, ig   ng   ns, would be a ridiculous distortion of   e fac   s virtually a democratic republic would b depict   very strong —though not quite an absolute—mona

The British constitutional system exists   oject to the legal sovereignty of parliament. No part   it has been incorporated in a document set above parliament, which parliament cannot alter, as the framework of the constitutional law of the United States is incorporated in the Constitution of the United States, which Congress cannot alter. The British system is therefore extremely flexible, subject to alteration in any of its parts by the ordinary process of parliamentary legislation. And since in the British system the courts recognize no law superior to an act of parliament, no judicial decision can override an act of parliament.

New York, N. Y.   R. L. S.
                                                        C. C. W.

BRITISH
CONSTITUTIONAL HISTORY
SINCE 1832

ROBERT LIVINGSTON SCHUYLER

Gouverneur Morris Professor Emeritus of History
Columbia University

AND

CORINNE COMSTOCK WESTON

Associate Professor of History
University of Houston

AN ANVIL ORIGINAL
under the general editorship of
LOUIS L. SNYDER

D. VAN NOSTRAND COMPANY, INC.
PRINCETON, NEW JERSEY
TORONTO   LONDON
NEW YORK

D. VAN NOSTRAND COMPANY, INC.

120 Alexander St., Princeton, New Jersey
257 Fourth Avenue, New York 10, New York
25 Hollinger Rd., Toronto 16, Canada
Macmillan & Co., Ltd., St. Martin's St.,
London, W.C. 2, England

*All correspondence should be addressed to the
principal office of the company at Princeton, N. J.*

Library of Congress Catalog Card No. 56-12903

TABLE OF CONTENTS

Part I

BRITISH CONSTITUTIONAL HISTORY SINCE 1832

— 1 —

INTRODUCTION: MIXED GOVERNMENT AND DEMOCRACY BEFORE 1832

English Political Principles and Constitutional Practices. In any constitutional system governmental powers are exercised in accordance with accepted principles and assumptions derived from some sort of underlying political philosophy. If the political philosophy changes, and with it the constitutional assumptions, the exercise of governmental powers cannot remain unaffected, and throughout the long course of English constitutional history prevailing political principles have been reflected in constitutional practice. An illustration in point has been the use of ancient royal prerogative powers, which originally implied no suggestion of democracy, as modern instruments of democracy. The British Queen now reigning possesses most of the legal powers of her autocratic predecessors—of Henry VIII, Charles I, James II—but she does not possess personal discretion in the exercise of these powers. If we look to the letter of the law only, Britain is today not, indeed, an absolute monarchy, but a very strong monarchy. If, however, we look to recognized constitutional practices and conventions, it is better described as a crowned republic. The great powers of the crown must be exercised in accordance with what is now the fundamental assumption of the constitution, namely, the principle of democracy.

Democracy, however, has not always been the fundamental principle of the English constitution. It did not become so until well into the nineteenth century, not until the Reform Act of 1832 had revealed its tendencies, and its tendencies were not immediately apparent even to its own authors. It took time for the far-reaching effects of the great reform of 1832 to work their way into popular consciousness. For, as Walter Bagehot pointed out in his famous *English Constitution,* published a generation after the Reform Act was passed, a new constitution does not produce its full effect as long as it continues to be worked by statesmen who were trained under an older constitution, and the statesmen who remained at the helm in Britain during the generation following 1832—Lord John Russell, Lord Palmerston, Lord Derby —had grown up and served their apprenticeship in politics under the old, pre-1832, régime. And furthermore— and this, too, Bagehot remarked—paper descriptions of the constitution, what he called "the literary theory of the constitution," have always tended to be out of date, have been, indeed, more or less out of date even when they were written, because "when a great entity like the British Constitution has continued in connected outward sameness, but hidden inner change, for many ages, every generation inherits a series of inapt words, of maxims once true but of which the truth is ceasing or has ceased."

One of the most important and influential parts of what Bagehot called the literary theory of the constitution was the theory of mixed government, or the theory of checks and balances, often spoken of as the classical theory of the English constitution. This theory held sway from the Restoration in 1660 until after the Reform Act of 1832, a period longer than that during which the theory of democracy has been generally accepted. According to Bagehot:

. . . it is insisted that the peculiar excellence of the British Constitution lies in a balanced union of three powers. It is said that the monarchical element, the aristocratic element, and the democratic element, have each a share in the supreme sovereignty, and that the assent of all three is necessary to the action of that sovereignty. King, lords, and commons, by this theory, are alleged to be not only the outward form, but the inner moving essence, the vitality of the constitution.

Mixed Government and the English Constitution. The virtues of mixed government were celebrated in ancient times, especially by the historian Polybius. Aristotle in his *Politics* had discussed and distinguished between three types of "pure," or unmixed, government—monarchy, aristocracy, and democracy—and had referred to instances of mixed government. Polybius, who attributed the advance of Rome to her dominant position in the Mediterranean world primarily to Roman political institutions, looked upon the Roman constitution as the outstanding example of a mixture of the three elements. The "pure" forms of government were, he believed, of evil tendency: pure monarchy tended to degenerate into tyranny, pure aristocracy into oligarchy, and pure democracy into mob rule. Fortunate Rome blended and balanced the three elements in such a happy combination that the tendencies to degeneration inherent in each, in its pure form, were canceled.

The opinion that the English constitution represented this same meritorious mixture of monarchy, aristocracy, and democracy seems to have originated in Tudor England. But even before that, as early, seemingly, as there was any theorizing to speak of in England regarding the nature of English government, the view was expressed that it was a mixed government. This was the opinion of Sir John Fortescue, Chief Justice of the Court of King's Bench in the reign of Henry VI, a sturdy English nationalist and author of the earliest treatises to deal with the English constitution, as distinguished from English law. Fortescue found a mixture of a kind, though not quite the later triple mixture, in the governmental system of his day. He distinguished between what he called *dominium politicum et regale,* a form of mixed government of which the English government was an example, and *dominium regale,* the type to which the government of France belonged; and, patriotic Englishman that he was, he exalted the former in comparison with the latter. Whatever the French king was, the English king, in Fortescue's thought, was a decidedly limited monarch. Fortescue's conception of *dominium politicum et regale* was not original with him, but he did a good deal to associate it with the English form of government, and he has his place in the evolution of the theory of English mixed government.

The earliest expressions of the view that the English constitution represented a mixture of the monarchic,

aristocratic, and democratic principles come to us from
the second half of the sixteenth century. The best-known
treatise on English government written during this period
was Sir Thomas Smith's *De Republica Anglorum*. Smith
regarded the government of England as mixed, and we
may consider the three-fold mixture as implied in his
statement, which has often been quoted, that the supreme
power in England resided in parliament, for parliament,
as he used the term, meant king, lords, and commons.
A more explicit statement that the English mixture was
the same blend of monarchic, aristocratic, and democratic
elements that Polybius had celebrated in ancient times
can be found in a tract written at the beginning of
Elizabeth I's reign by a clergyman named John Aylmer,
afterwards Bishop of London. Of like tenor was the view
expressed by another clergyman, John Ponet, later Bishop
of Winchester, in a tract written a few years before
Aylmer's.

Charles I's Answer to the Nineteen Propositions.
The most carefully formulated, as well as the most
authoritative and influential statement yet made of the
theory of mixed government as applied to the English
constitution, is to be found in Charles I's *Answer to the
Nineteen Propositions*, written in June, 1642, on the eve
of the English Civil War. *The Nineteen Propositions*,
which the Long Parliament had just presented to the King
as its ultimatum, is an easily accessible document; but
the King's *Answer*, though it was to have far greater
and more enduring influence on the course of later constitutional development than the *Nineteen Propositions*,
is not so easy to come by. It is not to be found in any
of the documentary compilations prepared for the use
of students of English constitutional history, nor is it
mentioned in the well-known textbooks. It is not to be
supposed, of course, that Charles I's *Answer* was written
by himself. It appears to have been drafted by two of
the moderate royalists who had recently accepted ministerial office under him, Viscount Falkland (Lucius
Cary) and Sir John (afterwards Baron) Colepeper, and
the paragraphs relating to mixed government were
probably drafted by Colepeper. These men were in no
sense supporters of the doctrine of the Divine Right of
Kings; as members of the Long Parliament they had

voted for the great measures of constitutional reform which that Parliament had recently enacted.

The King's *Answer* cannot be interpreted so as to make it consistent with divine-right monarchy, the political-religious theory in which Charles I had been brought up. Whether or not he had honestly abandoned that theory, there is no trace of it in his *Answer*. Whatever may have been in the inmost recesses of his mind, the unquestionable fact is that in this document, to which wide publicity was given by his order, he took his stand on the doctrine of mixed government, which, as we have seen, had been advanced in the Tudor period. The government of England, it was now declared by authority of the King himself, was a mixture of monarchy, aristocracy, and democracy, represented respectively by the King, the House of Lords, and the House of Commons, a mixture which gave England all the advantages of monarchy, aristocracy, and democracy, without any of their disadvantages, as long as the balance was maintained among king, lords, and commons. The *Nineteen Propositions*, if they had been accepted by the King and put into practice, would have destroyed that balance, and it was on this ground that the King rejected them. The monarchical element in the constitution would, in effect, have disappeared. (*See Reading No. 1.*)

Democracy in the Puritan Revolution. In the period of the civil wars (1642-1648) there developed a democratic movement which rejected the principles of mixed government, exalted the House of Commons as the representative of the people, and advocated the abolition of the monarchy and the House of Lords. It arose within radical groups among the Independents (themselves radical religious groups among the Puritans) who were spoken of as Levellers and whose best-known leader was John Lilburne. Democracy in the Puritan Revolution was thus a product of "the dissidence of dissent," to borrow a phrase of Edmund Burke's, and it was in origin a political-theological theory, in this respect resembling the doctrine of the Divine Right of Kings. The Leveller movement made rapid headway in the rank and file of the Long Parliament's New Model Army, and Leveller proposals for constitutional reorganization were set forth in documents known as Agreements of the

People. The last of these, sponsored by the Army, was presented to the so-called Rump Parliament shortly before the execution of the King in January, 1649. It was a republican plan, under which there would have been no King or House of Lords, but no action was taken on it.

What sealed the King's fate, and for the time being the fate of mixed government, was the Second Civil War, in 1648. Following the final defeat of the royalist forces, the moderate-royalist Presbyterian members of the House of Commons of the Long Parliament were excluded (by the military *coup d'état* known as Pride's Purge), the Independents, supported by the Army, came into complete political control, and the Army officers, even the more conservative among them (most notably Oliver Cromwell and his son-in-law Henry Ireton), were converted to republicanism, though not to all the radical demands of the Levellers.

An ordinance for the establishment of a tribunal to try the King was passed by what was left of the House of Commons (known in English history as the Rump Parliament), but it was rejected by a remnant of the House of Lords, whereupon the Commons, in January, 1649, passed the following resolutions, which signified rejection of the theory of mixed government and acceptance of the principle of democracy:

That the People are, under God, the original of all just power.

That the Commons of England, in Parliament assembled, being chosen by and representing the People, have the supreme power in this nation.

That whatsoever is enacted, or declared for law by the Commons, in Parliament assembled, hath the force of law; and all the people of this nation are concluded thereby, although the consent and concurrence of King, or House of Peers, be not had thereunto.

The Rump then proceeded to pass an act establishing a tribunal to try the King, and following his execution in January, 1649, it quickly swept away the institutions of mixed government. In March it abolished the office of king as "unnecessary, burdensome, and dangerous to the liberty, safety, and public interest of the people," and two days later it abolished the House of Lords as "useless and dangerous to the people of England." Two months after that, on May 19, the Rump declared that "the people of England, and of all the dominions and territories thereunto belonging" were "a commonwealth and free state," and were to be governed by "the supreme authority of this nation—the representatives of the people in parliament, and by such as they shall appoint and constitute as officers and ministers under them for the good of the people, and that without any king or house of lords."

For the time being, mixed government had disappeared, but the Puritan experiment in theoretical democracy, which depended actually upon the very undemocratic Rump Parliament and the support of the Army and had no basis in popular approval, proved short-lived. Cromwell disposed of the Rump by a military *coup d'état* in 1653, and under a written constitution known as the Instrument of Government, which represented the ideas of a group of Army officers and was imposed on the country by military power, he became head of the state with the title of Lord Protector. As such he restored a monarchical element, though not the name of king, to the constitution. He went further in restoring mixed government when he accepted amendments to the Instrument of Government which provided for the establishment of a new second chamber. This latter, known as "the other House," was set up and was thought of by contemporaries as occupying a position similar to that of the old House of Lords. It was the result of discontent with the experiment of a single-chamber legislature, but it was short-lived, for it did not come into existence until the Puritan régime was approaching its fall.

The Restoration.   With the Restoration, the Puritan experiments in government were swept away, and the Puritan theory of democracy was abandoned. An act of 1660 declared by implication that all the parliamentary enactments from the time of the breach between the king and the houses of parliament in 1642 were invalid, and an act of 1661 expressly declared them null and void. What was restored at the Restoration, however, was not the autocracy of Charles I's personal government as it had worked before the meeting of the Long Parliament in 1640. The great constitutional reforms

accomplished in the early sessions of that parliament
were not undone. Ship money and other forms of royal
taxation, without the consent of parliament, were not
restored, nor were the Star Chamber and other prerogative courts which had been abolished. What was restored,
so the men of the Restoration believed, was the system of
mixed government, now venerated because of its association with the name of the martyred King, the system
outlined in his *Answer to the Nineteen Propositions*, to
which frequent reference was made, the system then
often spoken of as "The King's Constitution." The pros-
perous course run by the theory of mixed government
during the half-dozen generations following the Restoration is explained, in part at least, by the fate that had be-
fallen it, for the time being, in the hurricane of the
Puritan Revolution.

Mixed Government after the Restoration.   Between
the Restoration in 1660 and the Reform Act of 1832
there was general acceptance of the mixed-government
theory of the English constitution. In the pamphlet literature inspired by the Revolution of 1688 frequent reference was made to Charles I's *Answer to the Nineteen
Propositions*. Not everybody was satisfied with the way
in which the constitutional system was working in practice. There were what may be called mixed-government
reformers, who thought that the system of mixed government, with its checks and balances, could and should
be improved and strengthened; and, beginning in the
last decade of the eighteenth century and under the influence of the French Revolution, there were a few
democratic reformers who were opposed to the theory
of mixed government and believed that it ought to be
abandoned in favor of democracy. Both classes of reformers, however, were in agreement in viewing mixed
government as the ruling principle of the existing constitution. And the same view was held by statesmen,
whether reformers or not, and by writers who under-
took to expound and interpret the constitution. Among
the latter was Sir William Blackstone in his famous and
vastly influential *Commentaries on the Laws of England*
(1765), long to serve as the basis of legal education
throughout the English-speaking world. (*See Reading
No. 2.*)

Mixed Government and the Lords. Among the mixed-government reformers were a few—not very numerous—who advocated reform of the House of Lords in the eighteenth and early nineteenth centuries. From the modern democratic point of view, reform of the House of Lords means making it more popular and less aristocratic in character, but this was not the object of those who proposed House of Lords reform before 1832. The student of history always needs to be on guard against the anachronism of reading the ideas and viewpoints of his own day too far back into the past, and here is a case in point. What animated would-be reformers of the House of Lords in the eighteenth and early nineteenth centuries was not a desire to democratize it or to diminish its powers, but rather a wish to strengthen it with a view to enabling it the better to play the role assigned to it in the theory of mixed government. Proposals to reform the House of Lords within the framework of mixed government included the following: (1) limitation of the power of the crown to create new peers, notably in the Peerage Bill of 1719, which, though it did not become law, gave rise to much discussion and controversy, and which was avowedly intended to free the House of Lords from undue royal and ministerial influence; (2) exclusion of the bishops of the Church of England and the Scottish peers from the House of Lords, the former being royal appointees and the latter much under ministerial influence; (3) creation of life peers, with the object of strengthening the House of Lords in its relation both to the House of Commons and to the crown; and (4) the establishment of property qualifications for membership in the Lords, on the ground that wealth was necessary to enable the House to play its proper role.

Mixed Government and the Commons. The question of the reform of the House of Commons (theoretically the democratic branch of the government), which was advocated by a number of writers in the second half of the eighteenth century, has attracted a good deal of historical interest, but here, too, anachronism has been at work to cause misinterpretation. The subject has been regarded too much from the modern democratic point of view, without appreciation of its setting in the context of contemporary mixed-government theory. Looked at from this modern standpoint, it seems strange that the eighteenth-century parliamentary reformers, who were so eager to democratize the House of Commons, did not find fault with the undemocratic House of Lords. But granting their premises and assumptions, there was really nothing strange about it. The reason why political reformers before 1832, with only a very few exceptions, made no serious criticism of the House of Lords was that they accepted the mixed-government theory of the English constitution and the imporant role assigned in that theory to the House of Lords as a balancing force, mediating between crown and commons and preserving an equilibrium in the constitutional system. They did not attack the undemocratic House of Lords for the simple reason that they were not democrats, pure and simple, but rather what might be called "mixed democrats." To their minds, the House of Lords, representing the aristocratic principle, was an essential part of mixed government, and it ought to remain aristocratic. Not until the days of the French Revolution did English reformers advocate the abolition of the House of Lords or even steps toward democratizing it; and even then only a few of them did so. They had little or no influence on the ideas of the governing classes or on the course of political events.

Parliamentary Reform. The organized movement for House of Commons reform—parliamentary reform, as historians generally have called it—got under way as a result of the celebrated Wilkes Affair, in 1769. When the House of Commons, dominated by court and ministerial influence and no longer content with refusing John Wilkes the seat to which the electors of Middlesex County had persistently elected him, gave the seat to a candidate who had received fewer votes than Wilkes, it struck directly at its own representative character. It thus raised the issue of the People *versus* the House of Commons. Radical societies were organized for House of Commons reform, and a radical party came into being—radical but not democratic in our sense of the word.

Among the reforms for which the radicals agitated were the elimination from the electoral system of the small boroughs which lent themselves to manipulation by borough patrons or by the government and, in some cases, to cruder forms of bribery; the division of the country into constituencies approximately equal in population; the extension of the franchise; the subordination of members of the House of Commons to their constituents; the exclusion of officeholders from the House; and more frequent parliamentary elections. To modern ears all this sounds thoroughly democratic, but to the radicals themselves the sound was different. One of them was the Duke of Richmond, who in 1780 introduced a bill, which was not passed, providing for universal manhood suffrage, equal electoral districts, and annual parliaments—a favorite trio with the reformers. In a very illuminating letter written later, which seems to have enjoyed high repute in the reform societies, he explicitly denied that he was in favor of democratic government. What he desired, he said, was to preserve the admirable system of mixed government. (*See Reading No. 3.*)

Not all of these who advocated reform within the framework of mixed government were found within the ranks of the radicals. Edmund Burke is an outstanding case in point. As the intellectual leader of one of the factions of the Whig party, he was a strong critic of George III in his efforts to rule through the manipulation of parliaments and elections, during the dozen years (1770-1782) in which Great Britain experienced the humiliation of the loss of most of her old empire as a result of the American Revolution. To Burke's mind, crown and ministerial influence over the House of Commons, exerted through the distribution of the patronage and the dispensing of other royal favors, was the main threat to the constitution. He believed, in the often-quoted words of a resolution passed by the House of Commons in 1780, that "the influence of the Crown has increased, is increasing, and ought to be diminished," and he was the principal sponsor of legislation passed in 1782 that had the effect of reducing that influence substantially. But with Burke, circumstances always altered cases, and there was no reason why a statesman who regarded monarchical influence as the greatest menace to constitutional stability in 1780 should not have

viewed democratic power in that same light ten years
later, as Burke actually did, the French Revolution having given him in the meantime a fear of the masses and
a dread of the spread of revolutionary ideas among them.

Democratic Reformers. The French Revolution
has been called the most important event in English
history. However that may be, it certainly had much to
do with introducing into the movement for reform in
England the principle of democracy, or perhaps we
should say (remembering the Leveller movement in the
seventeenth century) with reintroducing it. The virtues
of democratic republicanism had been pointed out in
controversial writings in the days of the American Revolution—notably in the most influential of all of them,
Thomas Paine's *Common Sense.* But Paine was then
writing as an American partisan, not as a reformer of
English government. The desirability of preserving mixed
government in England does not appear to have been
seriously questioned before the French Revolution.

In the early 1790's, however, three books were published in which the principles of mixed government were
vigorously attacked. Their authors were democrats, pure
and unmixed, and the form of government which they
preferred was republican. All three of them—Joseph
Priestley, Thomas Paine, and William Godwin—had
much in common. They were all profoundly influenced
by the revolutionary movements in America and France
which, to their minds, ushered in a new and glorious era
in human history. They were true sons of the Enlightenment, for whom the idea of progress, unlimited confidence in the efficacy of human reason, and belief in the
perfectibility of mankind had all the appeal of religious
dogma. As was generally true of reformers of the natu-
ral-rights school, the cast of their minds was absolutist,
and they had little or no sense of relativity in politics or
history. They had a common background of religious
dissent, between which and democratic republicanism
there was an historical affinity—the two had gone hand
in hand during the Puritan Revolution. More important,
there was also a natural affinity, since dissenters in
eighteenth-century England were subject to various disabilities which predisposed them to political discontent
and criticism of the *status quo* in general. Priestley was

a Unitarian, and Unitarians were not entitled under the law to the toleration granted to Trinitarian dissenters by the Toleration Act of 1689. Paine was a Deist of Quaker antecedents, altogether outside the Christian fold, to whom all established churches and all political inequalities were anathema. Godwin, for a time a dissenting minister, moved from dissent to agnosticism or atheism. The writings in which these three democrats gave expression to their opinions regarding the English government were Priestley's *A Political Dialogue on the General Principles of Government* (1791), Paine's *The Rights of Man*, in two parts (1791 and 1792, respectively), and Godwin's *Enquiry concerning Political Justice and Its Influence on Morals* (1793).

Priestley. In earlier writings Priestley had praised the English system of mixed government, which he then considered to be the best form of polity. But under the influence of new revolutionary constitutions abroad his opinions were altered. In the *Political Dialogue* he stated frankly that he had changed his mind about the English constitution. He now objected on principle to an hereditary monarchy and an hereditary legislative chamber and attacked the whole theory of checks and balances. He outlined a democratic plan of government for Great Britain, in which the chief executive was to be elected and the second chamber, if there were one, would have only a suspensive veto on legislation.

Paine. Paine was a more effective and influential propagandist for democracy than Priestley, and the government was more afraid of him. His *Rights of Man* (one of the many published replies to Burke's *Reflections on the Revolution in France*) had a huge sale in England, as his *Common Sense* had had fifteen years before in America. In this, Paine attacked the theory and practice of mixed government (*see Reading No. 4*), and he also denounced the House of Lords as representing the principle of checks and balances. Radical societies, especially the London Corresponding Society, founded in 1792 under the leadership of Thomas Hardy, a politically minded shoemaker, spread Paine's writings, though the extent to which his republicanism was adopted by members of the societies can easily be exaggerated. Hardy was one of a number of members of the radical societies who were tried for treason in 1794 on the charge of attempting to set up a republic in England, but the government's efforts to convict them failed. The course of the French Revolution, leading as it did to military dictatorship, gravely discredited English radicalism and gave it a severe set-back, and by the end of the eighteenth century the radical societies had practically expired. Paine's ideas, however, were not permanently buried. In 1816 a young journeyman tinsmith, Richard Carlile, read *The Rights of Man* and was forthwith converted to republicanism. Two years later he was instrumental in having Paine's writings republished, which was the principal reason for his being sentenced to imprisonment in Dorchester Jail. Here he began the publication of an underground periodical, *The Republican,* which did much to keep Paine's ideas alive, especially among the working classes. On the eve of the great Reform Bill of 1832, Carlile was diffusing his republican propaganda in lectures at the Rotunda, a London music hall, where persons later associated with the working-class movement known as Chartism also lectured. It seems probable that Paine's republicanism passed through Carlile into the politics of the working classes in the large towns and had an influence on the Chartist movement, to which reference will be made in the next chapter.

Godwin. Godwin was the most radical of the three democratic reformers of the 1790's. He was not only a democrat; he was a theoretical anarchist. Nor did he confine his opposition to existing political institutions; he attacked private property, and he disapproved of marriage as an institution. He not only believed that government was inherently evil, but he hopefully anticipated that it would wither away with the progress of human enlightenment. Hereditary institutions could not be reconciled with the principle of equality; and political justice, based upon equality, could not result from combining hereditary monarchy and hereditary aristocracy with democracy. The vaunted English mixed-government constitution thus stood condemned on its own face. Godwin was perhaps the most doctrinaire of all the eighteenth-century English radical reformers, though that is saying a good deal, and he was never troubled by doubts as to his own omniscience. Godwin's *Political Justice* was published at a high price (three guineas), beyond the reach of individuals in the poorer classes, but working-men banded together for its purchase and for reading it aloud; and it has been estimated that some 4000 copies of the original edition were sold, and a cheaper edition was brought out in 1796. It is of some significance that the work was republished in 1843, when the Chartist movement was at its height, and it is known that the Chartists made some use of it.

Cartwright.   Two more reformers should be mentioned—both of them converted to pure and unmixed democracy in the early nineteenth century, before the Reform Bill of 1832. One was the veteran radical John Cartwright, whose earlier efforts to promote parliamentary reform, beginning in 1776, had been confined to democratizing the House of Commons, with the avowed object of strengthening the system of mixed government. He had not attacked either hereditary monarchy or the hereditary aristocratic House of Lords, with its right of absolute veto on bills passed by the House of Commons. On the contrary, he had attributed to the House of Lords an indispensable function in mixed government, that of holding the balance between the monarch and the people. But in the course of time this mixed democrat, as in Priestley's case, became a pure democrat. In *The English Constitution Produced and Illustrated* (1823), written when he was well along in his eighties, he held the House of Lords up to public ridicule and condemnation and spoke of "the unnatural practice, the false policy, and the glaring injustice of hereditary royalty." After the manner of most reformers in his day—and some in ours—Cartwright had a lively distrust of what Burke called "the desperate enterprises of innovation." He thought of the reforms he advocated as a restoration or a renovation, not an innovation, and he convinced himself that in the good old days (in this case the Anglo-Saxon period of English history) England had actually enjoyed a democratic constitution. His pamphlet, which was written in the form of dialogues, seems to have had no large sale, and its influence was not great.

Bentham.   In the history of English reform in gen-

eral, Jeremy Bentham holds a much more important position than Cartwright or, indeed, than any of the other
reformers we have spoken of, though constitutional
reform represented only one phase of his long-continued
efforts to promote human happiness. The intellectual
father of what came to be called Utilitarianism, or
Philosophic Radicalism, Bentham did not keep company
with radicals in his early days. He was repelled by their
appeals to natural law, in the existence of which (in the
juristic sense) he did not believe, and he was not then
deeply interested in the subjects which so greatly interested them. It was, however, in one of their writings,
Priestley's *Essay on the First Principles of Government*
(1768), that he found what became the master principle
of his social, legal, political, and ethical philosophy—
namely, that the greatest happiness of the greatest number is the test that ought to be applied to all human
institutions and laws. And this test, when applied candidly
to the institutions of England in Bentham's day, was
likely to breed reformers fully as radical as those who
appealed to the law of nature and the inherent rights
of man.

Bentham's influence has perhaps been greatest in the
field of law reform, but in time he became a parliamentary
reformer as well. His opinions as such were not published
until well into the nineteenth century—in his *Plan of
Parliamentary Reform*, which appeared in 1818, when
he was seventy, his *On Houses of Peers and Senates*,
published in 1830, and his *Constitutional Code*, not
published in full until some years after his death in 1832,
though the ideas it expressed had no doubt already been
discussed in Benthamite circles. The old reformer had
come to the conclusion that nothing effective in the way
of reform was to be hoped for in England under its
mixed-government constitution, and that the governing
classes were interested only in promoting their own interests and would not work for his ideal, the greatest
happiness of the greatest number. Theoretically, an enlightened despotism might aim at the greatest happiness
of the greatest number, but the monarchy of George III
in his declining years, of the Regency, and of George IV
was neither enlightened nor despotic; and it would have
required high powers of imagination to conceive of the

members of the House of Lords as trustees for the people.
Neither the monarchy nor the House of Lords was to
Bentham's mind consistent with the greatest happiness
principle, and it was clear to him that both ought to be
abolished. Mere reform of the House of Commons,
Bentham came to believe, would be useless if the monarchy and the House of Lords were allowed to continue.
(*See Reading No. 5.*) He not only condemned the existing House of Lords root and branch, but he was opposed to a second chamber of any kind. Bentham's
rejection of the principle of mixed government and
advocacy of democracy were well known in Benthamite
circles before 1832 and continued to influence his followers after 1832. It is worthy of note that serious
criticism of the House of Lords and proposals for its
reform that were made after the passing of the Reform
Act of 1832 came mainly from individuals who had
been influenced by Bentham's teachings.

It appears, then, that a number of reformers advocated
genuinely democratic reforms in the English constitutional system before 1832, men who were not content
with reform of the House of Commons within the framework of mixed government but attacked the principle
of mixed government itself. Priestley, Paine, Godwin,
Cartwright, and Bentham have been mentioned, and
Paine and Bentham at least had disciples. Yet it would
be a mistake to think that the ideas of these men had
much influence on effective public opinion before 1832.
So far as the governing classes at least were concerned,
both Whigs and Tories thought of themselves, in the
crisis of the Reform Bill, as champions of the old and
long-lauded theory of mixed government, with its system of checks and balances. The Whigs claimed that
they had come to fulfill the old constitution, not to
destroy it, that the Bill was necessary for strengthening
and preserving mixed government. The Tories predicted
that it would prove fatal to the old system. The Tories
were the better prophets.

— 2 —

FROM MIXED GOVERNMENT TO DEMOCRACY, 1832-1867

Significance of the Great Reform Bill. The Great Reform Bill, passed in 1832 after prolonged and unprecedented public excitement and agitation, is always regarded as one of the conspicuous landmarks in English constitutional history. To understand why this is so, it is necessary to recall the circumstances surrounding the passing of the Bill. Its full constitutional significance is not revealed in its particular provisions, nor in its avowed purposes. The Bill itself did not involve any departure from the old principles of mixed government. The Whig statesmen who championed it were not democrats in our sense of the word. (*See Reading No. 6.*) Nor, of course, were their Tory opponents. Whigs and Tories vied with each other in professing devotion to the doctrine of mixed government, and both parties regarded the word "democrat" as a term of reproach. To them democracy suggested mob rule, the triumph of poverty over wealth and of ignorance over knowledge. Members of the aristocracy or closely affiliated with it, the Whig leaders claimed to be the real friends of the old system of mixed government and contended that the Bill would result in preserving and strengthening it. The Tory opponents of the Bill, predicting that it would lead to the eventual destruction of mixed government in favor of democracy (*see Reading No. 7*), were better prophets than the Whigs. And as prophets, the advocates of genuine democracy, both in the middle classes and in the working classes, agreed with the Tories; for the most part they strenuously supported the Bill, even though it fell short of their ideals, because they regarded it as the first step toward thorough-going democracy.

The great importance of the Reform Bill, as has been well said, "proved in the end to be less in the immediate change it made than in introducing the possibility of change." It was in the mode of its passing, and in its consequences, rather than in its actual provisions, that it dealt a body blow to the old theory of the three co-ordinate factors in government—monarchy, aristocracy, and democracy—balancing one another in the general interest. The old theory, however, was a long time dying, and throughout the years 1832-1867, though developments in the direction of democracy were actually taking place, statesmen continued to profess loyalty to it.

Prelude to Reform. When the Whigs formed a ministry in 1830, parliamentary reform, as an immediate political issue, was in the air. The long struggle with Revolutionary France and Napoleon (1793-1815), which had discouraged earlier movements for reform in Britain, had come to an end at Waterloo, and almost everybody regarded some measure of reform as necessary. In November, 1830, the Ministry of the Tory Duke of Wellington was defeated in the House of Commons and resigned. William IV asked the Whig leader Earl Grey to form a ministry. Grey, who had advocated parliamentary reform within the structure of mixed government forty years before, accepted the King's commission. He believed that an extensive, though not radical, measure of reform was called for, a measure "large enough to satisfy public opinion" and "to afford sure ground of resistance to further innovation," and on March 1, 1831, the Reform Bill was introduced in the House of Commons by Lord John Russell.

The Reform Bill in Parliament. After a long and exciting debate the Bill passed its second reading, but by a majority of only one vote, virtually a defeat for the Ministry because it was not sufficient to insure the final passing of the Bill. The Cabinet, impressed by widespread public demonstrations in support of the Bill, was in favor of dissolving parliament and appealing to the country in a general election, and the King acquiesced, though reluctantly, because he was anxious to avoid public clamor and dissension over the question of parliamentary reform. Parliament was dissolved in April, 1831. The general election which ensued aroused unprecedented excitement. It was a great victory for the reformers. In July a second Bill, differing from the first only in certain details, was passed at its second reading in the new House of Commons by a majority of 136. The House of Lords rejected it, however, early in October by a majority of 41 in a vote of 357, and shortly thereafter the King, on the advice of the Cabinet, put an end to the session by proroguing parliament.

Public Agitation. In the interval between this and the opening of the new session public excitement rose to extraordinary and even dangerous heights, as evidenced in the press and by petitions, mass meetings, and even rioting in many cities by radical supporters of the Bill. A third Bill was introduced in the new session, passed by the House of Commons in March, 1832, and sent to the Lords, where it passed second reading on April 14 by a majority of 9. But on May 7 an amendment to the Bill was carried in the Lords against the Ministry. "The Days of May" is the name that was given to the short period of eleven days that followed this action.

William IV and the Whig Ministry. It was widely believed that the King had agreed to create a sufficient number of peers to carry the Bill through the Lords if that should be necessary to save it, though it appears that he had probably not committed himself to such an indefinite creation. On May 8 the Cabinet decided to resign unless the King would agree to create enough peers to insure the success of the Bill in all its essentials. The next day he refused to give such an assurance and accepted the resignation of his Whig ministers. The immediate question then was whether the Tories could form a ministry capable of governing and of carrying through parliament some measure of parliamentary reform, which everyone now recognized to be necessary. The Duke of Wellington sounded out other Tory leaders, but after a few days he had to inform the King that his efforts had failed. A Tory ministry under existing conditions, with the Whigs in a large majority in the House of Commons, was not practicable, and he advised the King to recall Grey and his colleagues, who had remained in office pending the appointment of their successors. On May 18 the Whig Cabinet asked for "full and indisputable security" to carry the Reform Bill. There being no other course open to the King, he yielded and gave what amounted to a promise to create as many peers as might be necessary to insure the passing of the Bill by the House of Lords. As it turned out, it was not necessary to create peers. The threat that this would be done if need be was sufficient. The Lords yielded and allowed the Bill to pass with trifling amendments which were accepted by the House of Commons. It became law on June 7, 1832.

The Reform Bill in Relation to Mixed Government and Democracy. The provisions of the Reform Bill themselves—the disfranchisement of so-called "pocket" and "rotten" boroughs, the enfranchisement of newer industrial and commercial towns, an increase in the representation of the counties, and a cautious and far from radical extension of the parliamentary franchise— were not incompatible with the old theory of mixed government. But what could not be reconciled with the old theory was the way in which the Bill had been passed. In a great constitutional crisis that theory broke down. The House of Commons and the Ministry which it supported won a great victory, and the King and the House of Lords suffered a great defeat. Among the political leaders of the country there were men who understood the meaning of what had occurred. In a re- markably perceptive private letter, written on the mor- row of the crisis, in December, 1832, the Duke of Well- ington said:

. . . there is no reflecting man who in looking at the trans- actions of that time will not see that the Reform Bill was carried . . . by the Ministers and the House of Commons against the King and the House of Lords. It is true that the King and the House of Lords were saved at that moment, the former from disgrace, and the latter from being swamped. But I cannot consider either at present as in a state of inde- pendence.

In terms of mixed government Wellington was saying that the democratic branch of the government, in this constitutional crisis, had successfully asserted its superi- ority to the monarchical and aristocratic branches.

The Old Representative System. Before consider- ing the more important provisions of the Reform Act, something needs to be said about representation in parlia- ment as it existed before 1832. The House of Commons,

which came into existence in the Middle Ages, was so
named because it represented organized communities,
the counties and boroughs of England; and the word
commons came to be used to designate the representatives of those communities in parliament. Each county
and each borough was originally supposed to elect two
representatives, irrespective of its population or wealth,
for it was communities as corporate entities, not mere
aggregations of people and property, that were to be
represented. By no means did all the boroughs send members to the House of Commons, and the number of
those that did so came to be fixed. No change took place
between the seventeenth century and 1832. During this
period, however, there were great changes in the distribution of population and wealth, especially during what
came to be known as the Industrial Revolution. Many
old and once flourishing boroughs declined, and many
towns which were not parliamentary boroughs became
important industrial and commercial centers. But of these
changes no account was taken for purposes of parliamentary representation. An important feature of the old
representative system, and one that did not wholly disap-
pear in 1832, was the existence of proprietary or "pocket"
boroughs, for which members were virtually appointed
by borough patrons, usually peers or other large landowners, whose local influence was such as to insure the
return of their nominees. Many of these patrons were
themselves subject to government influence of one kind
or another. There were also boroughs in which the government had a direct control through its influence over
officeholders living in these boroughs; there were "rotten" boroughs, in which the voters were notoriously
subject to bribery and seats were bought; and there were
"open" boroughs, in which more democratic conditions
existed. Early in the nineteenth century probably half
of the members of the House of Commons were the
nominees of patrons.

The Parliamentary Franchise before 1832. As to
the right to vote for members of the House of Commons,
a uniform county franchise was established in 1430 by
a statute which required the voter to be a resident of the
county in which he voted and in possession of a freehold
estate within it of an annual value of at least forty shil-

lings. The residence requirement fell into disuse and was at length abolished by statute in 1774, thus permitting non-resident and plural voting. The forty-shilling free-hold requirement, however, remained in effect till 1832. It was a very capricious requirement because there were other kinds of landholders than freeholders—copyhold-ers and leaseholders—and these were excluded from the franchise, no matter how valuable their estates. In the boroughs there was no uniformity in the parliamentary franchise before 1832. The right to vote depended on the borough charter and local usage. In some boroughs the franchise was fairly wide; in others, extremely nar-row. Neither in the boroughs nor in the counties did the possession of personal property, no matter of what value, give the right to vote. Thus it was not only the poor who were excluded from the parliamentary franchise before 1832. Many men of substance and wealth were excluded —manufacturers, merchants, bankers, and well-to-do landholders; and it was wealth, not poverty, that the Reform Act aimed to enfranchise. At a time when no provision had as yet been made for even the elementary instruction of the masses of the people, education was a virtual monopoly of the well-to-do, and ignorance and poverty went hand in hand.

Redistribution of Seats in 1832. The great Reform Act applied to England, including Wales. Corresponding acts were passed shortly afterwards for Scotland and Ireland. The more important provisions of these three acts were concerned with redistribution of seats in the House of Commons and changes in the parliamentary franchise. As to redistribution, in England fifty-six smaller boroughs were abolished as parliamentary con-stituencies and merged in the surrounding counties. In thirty boroughs the representation was reduced from two members each to one member. Forty-two parlia-mentary boroughs were created, of which twenty-two (including fourteen industrial towns in the midlands and the north of England) were to return two members each, and twenty, one member each. A considerable increase was made in county representation. Wales, Scotland, and Ireland were given slight increases in representation. Re-distribution in the Reform Acts of 1832 was not based upon the democratic principle of the representation of constituencies according to population. No attempt was made to divide the country into electoral districts equal in population, as had been advocated by radical reformers in the eighteenth century. The Reform Acts left the total number of seats in the House of Commons unchanged—658. The counties, however, gained in representation at the expense of the boroughs. Wales, Scotland, and Ireland gained slightly at the expense of England.

Extension of the Franchise in 1832. In considering changes in the franchise made in 1832 we have to distinguish between counties and boroughs because the qualifications for voting continued to differ widely as between the two. For the counties the old forty-shilling freehold qualification was modified. Under certain conditions the freehold, to qualify, must have an annual rental value of ten pounds (200 shillings), and some freeholders were actually disqualified. Much more important, however, was the admission to the franchise of other classes of landholders than freeholders. The right to vote was extended to copyholders of lands or tenements of an annual value of ten pounds or more; to leaseholders of lands or tenements of the same annual value or, in some cases, of fifty pounds or more; and to occupants of premises at an annual rent of fifty pounds or more, irrespective of the nature of the tenure. For all boroughs the legislation of 1832 established for the first time a uniform qualification, generally known as the ten-pound occupation franchise. In order to qualify, a man must occupy within the borough, as owner or tenant, a house, warehouse, counting-house, shop, or other building of the annual value of ten pounds or more, must have occupied such premises for at least twelve months prior to his registration, must have paid his taxes, and must have resided for at least six months within the borough or within seven miles thereof. (*See Reading No. 8.*)

The law regarding the parliamentary franchise, as has been seen, was extremely complicated and prolix; and it remained so down to 1918. The principle of universal manhood suffrage was not adopted. A man's right to vote—and prior to 1918 the right to vote was confined to adult male persons—depended upon his relation to property, and to real property, not personal property. It has been estimated that the Reform Acts of 1832 enfranchised somewhat less than 250,000 new voters, and they also disfranchised an appreciable number of old voters. Their beneficiaries were the middle classes in town and country. They left the working classes, urban and rural, still outside the electorate.

The Reformed House of Commons. The Reform Acts resulted in no drastic change in the social character of the House of Commons. The newly enfranchised voters did not choose other newly enfranchised voters to represent them. In the House of Commons elected in December, 1832 (the first general election after the passing of the Reform Acts) something like one-third of the members were sons of peers or baronets; and throughout the period 1832-1867 the prevailing tone of the House of Commons remained aristocratic. There was a marked difference in social position and public esteem between the average member of the House and the average ten-pound householder. England was still distinctly a land of social deference, a fact of much importance in the working of the constitutional system. It is not going too far to regard social deference as one of the pillars of the House of Commons and of the cabinet system as they existed during the generation following 1832. As was pointed out by Walter Bagehot in 1872, in the Introduction to the second edition of his *English Constitution,* "the mass of the 'ten-pound' householders did not really form their own opinions, and did not exact of their representatives an obedience to those opinions . . . they were in fact guided in their judgment by the better educated classes . . . they preferred representatives from those classes, and gave those representatives much license."

Working-Class Discontent. The next great measure of parliamentary reform after 1832 came a generation later, in 1867, though between these years the subject continued to be agitated. The working classes had cherished high hopes that the reforms of 1832 would lead to a great improvement in their economic and social conditions, and when this failed to take place, widespread disappointment and discontent were inevitable. The years immediately following the passing of the Reform Bill were marked by unusual legislative activity, and a number of important reform measures were enacted. Thus, in 1833 slavery was abolished throughout the British colonial empire by act of parliament; in the same year an important factory act was passed for the protection of children and young persons employed in textile industries; and the Municipal Corporations Act of 1835, a landmark in the history of English local government, provided for boroughs and cities (with some exceptions) a uniform and more orderly and efficient system of government. Such reforms, however, did not raise wages or lower the workingman's cost of living, and trade union activities, which were strongly opposed by employers of labor and by the government, were unsuccessful.

The Chartist Movement. It was in an atmosphere of grievance and disillusionment that the working-class movement known as Chartism had its origin. This comes within the scope of constitutional history because the Chartists agitated for parliamentary reforms beyond those of 1832, believing such reforms to be the necessary preliminary to economic and social reforms in the interests of the masses. Early in 1837 the London Working Men's Association, which had been founded in the preceding year and was followed by the formation of similar associations in other cities, decided to petition parliament for further parliamentary reforms. These were specified in the famous Six Points of "The People's Charter," a document published in May, 1837, in the form of a parliamentary bill. It contained a preamble, declaring that the House of Commons ought to represent accurately the wishes, feelings, and interests of the people, and the Six Points set forth in legal phraseology. These Six Points were: universal male suffrage, annual parliaments, vote by secret ballot, equal electoral districts, abolition of property qualifications for members of parliament, and payment of salaries to members of parliament. (*See Reading No. 9.*)

A petition in support of the Charter was presented to the House of Commons and gave rise to a debate on July 12, 1839, which resulted in the rejection of the petition by a vote of 235 to 46, whereupon a Chartist convention, then sitting in London, turned its attention to mobilizing the masses for more radical measures. Efforts to influence parliament were later renewed, however, and a second Chartist petition led to a debate in the House of Commons on May 3, 1842, which resulted in its rejection, 287 to 49. The collapse, a few months later, of a general strike in the north of England, centering in Manchester, greatly weakened the Chartist movement, which declined rapidly thereafter. The Chartists failed to obtain any of the parliamentary reforms they demanded, but their prolonged agitation forced upon the attention of thoughtful people in the middle and upper classes the widespread discontent that existed among the working classes. It led them to reflect on what Thomas Carlyle called "the condition-of-England question."

Abolition of Property Qualifications for Members of Parliament. One, though only one, of the Six Points was enacted into law during the period 1832-1867, namely, the abolition of property qualifications for members of parliament, and that was not until after Chartism itself had ceased to exist. These property qualifications had been imposed by act of parliament during the reign of Queen Anne and represented, at that time, a victory for the landed classes over the commercial and financial classes. The act required the possession of landed estates by all members of the House of Commons—estates worth 600 pounds a year in the case of county representatives, and 300 pounds in the case of borough representatives. In 1838 the law was modified by extending the qualification to include personal as well as real property, and in 1858 all provisions relating to the qualifications were repealed. In practice, however, this did not mean that poor men were able to sit in the House of Commons, for members of the House received no salaries at this time, nor did they until 1911. In fact, though no longer by law, membership in the House was confined to men of independent means.

Bagehot on the Cabinet. The first chapter of Walter Bagehot's *English Constitution*, written near the end of the period between the first and second Reform Act, is entitled "The Cabinet." Bagehot regarded the cabinet as "the most powerful body in the state," and looked upon it as the connecting link between the legislature and the executive, "a *hyphen* which joins, a *buckle* which fastens, the legislative part of the state to the executive part of the state." And the close union of executive and legislative powers he took to be "the efficient secret of the English Constitution," rejecting as erroneous the older view, associated particularly with the name of Montesquieu and still widely accepted in Bagehot's day, that the English constitution was characterized by a separation of governmental powers. Impressed by the dominant role played by the cabinet, Bagehot found it strange that so little was known about it. Its meetings were secret, and no official records of its proceedings were kept. "No description of it at once graphic and authentic," he said, "has ever been given." (*See Reading No. 10.*)

Extra-Legal Character of the Cabinet. Cabinets came into existence outside the realm of law, and what came to be spoken of as the cabinet system has always rested on conventions, not laws. No law has ever required the existence of a cabinet. The position of the prime minister, who is the head of the cabinet, was not recognized in any act of parliament before 1917 (the Chequers Estate Act), and the existence of ministers of cabinet rank was not recognized by parliament until the Ministers of the Crown Act was passed in 1937, which prescribed salaries for them. But this Act did not require the presence of such ministers at cabinet meetings, nor that such meetings should be held.

The Cabinet under Mixed Government. Cabinets developed in the early seventeenth century, probably as committees of the privy council, a body well known to the law that had come down from the Middle Ages and normally included the king's more important ministers. Cabinets never fitted well into the accepted theory of mixed government, and they were disliked from the first because of their secrecy, but an attempt to put an end to them in the Act of Settlement (1701) failed. Cabinets were small in membership, and their members enjoyed the special confidence of the sovereign, whom they assisted in determining matters of governmental policy. They were, also, as a rule, members of one house of parliament or the other, and leadership in parliament was an essential part of the functions they performed. This leadership was maintained by means of the royal and ministerial influence that resulted from the distribution to members of parliament of offices, pensions, government contracts, and other favors in the gift of the crown. The recipients of such royal favors could be counted on under normal conditions to support the king's government, as could the bulk of the more independent members of the House of Commons. It is not surprising that on only three occasions during the entire eighteenth century did the ministry of the day resign because it had lost its majority in the House of Commons, and such was the electoral influence of the crown and its friends among the borough patrons that no general election went against the ministry in office until after 1832.

Basic Characteristics of the Cabinet. It was only gradually that the cabinet acquired those characteristics which it has now long possessed: (1) political unanimity, (2) common, or collective, responsibility to parliament or, more accurately, to the House of Commons, (3) submission to a common head, the prime minister, and (4) the ultimate power of decision in all important questions of governmental policy, the sovereign being bound in practice to accept the cabinet's decision and give effect to it in so far as formal action by him was legally necessary to do so.

Political Unanimity. The political unanimity of the cabinet was not a recognized constitutional principle until after 1832. Differences of opinion within the cabinet had often been revealed to the sovereign, and there are instances of this long after 1832. Sometimes the sovereign asked for the individual opinions of cabinet members. Lord Grey's Cabinet, for example, was not unanimously in favor of creating peers to carry the Reform Bill in the House of Lords, a fact which strengthened William IV in his opposition to doing so. In the earlier stage of the crisis of 1832 the King, as we have seen, felt under no constitutional obligation to act in accordance with the wishes of the majority of his cabinet.

Collective Responsibility. And so it was with the principle of the collective responsibility of the cabinet to the House of Commons—a matter of gradual evolution. A distinction should be understood between the legal responsibility of individual ministers for their acts and the political responsibility of the cabinet as a whole for its policies. The former is much older than the latter.

Legal responsibility, the principle underlying the old procedure of impeachment, could be attributed only to individuals, not to a group which, as such, had no legal
existence, as was the case with the cabinet. The kind of
responsibility that could be, and gradually was, attributed to a cabinet was political responsibility to the
House of Commons. In the eighteenth century it was
found expedient on only a very few occasions for a ministry (and the cabinet was the core of the larger ministry)
to resign because it had lost the support of the House of
Commons, though the occasions were more numerous
when the sovereign made changes in the personnel of a
ministry out of deference to the wishes of the House of
Commons. As late as 1784, William Pitt, then Prime
Minister, rejected as contrary to the principles of the
English constitution the idea that ministers must resign
because the House of Commons disapproved of them.
Speaking in the House against an attempt by the majority to force his Ministry out of office, he declared that
this was contrary to constitutional principles, and his
speech showed that he was thinking within the framework of mixed government. He admitted that "a sentiment of disapprobation surely placed Ministers in awk-
ward and unpleasant situations; but that it should force
them to retire . . . was an unconstitutional doctrine,
hostile to the prerogative of the Crown, and to that balance of power on which the excellency of our government depended."

During the period 1832-1867 the House of Commons
exercised far greater control over the executive government than it had done in the eighteenth century or the
early part of the nineteenth. This is shown most strik-
ingly by the way in which ministries were terminated.
Between the accession of Queen Victoria in 1837 and
the resignation of the Russell-Gladstone Government in
1866 there were nine ministries, and each of them, with
only one exception, came to an end as a direct result of
an adverse vote in the House of Commons. (The single
exception was Lord Palmerston's second ministry, 1859-
1865, which was terminated by the death of the Prime
Minister.) The legal power of the sovereign to dismiss
ministers at pleasure was not abolished—and it never
has been—but it ceased to be exercised. That it became

customary for ministries to take their dismissal from the House of Commons is a fact of the utmost importance in the establishment of responsible government.

Twice during the first thirty years of the reign of Victoria the critical vote which led to the resignation of the ministry came at the opening of a new parliament, immediately following a general election in which a majority had been returned against the ministry. That is to say, the defeated ministry did not take its dismissal directly from the voters, but from the new House of Commons. This occurred in 1841, after the Conservatives had won a majority in an election in which the influence of the crown was strongly on the side of the Whig Ministry of Lord Melbourne, and in 1859, after a Liberal majority had been returned against Lord Derby's Conservative Ministry. For a general election to go against the ministry in office was something that had not happened before 1832, and Victoria, who in her early years as queen was intensely pro-Whig, looked upon the defeat of her Whig ministers in 1841 as a rebuff to the crown.

The Prime Minister. The prime minister has long been the most important and powerful figure in the English system of government. The position of prime minister, like the cabinet, of which he is the head, came into existence entirely outside the realm of law, and in its early days it was, like the cabinet, extremely unpopular. This seems to have been partly because the name was associated with the *premier ministre* in the French government and partly, no doubt, because such a position was not recognized in the accepted theory of mixed government. Sir Robert Walpole, who was first lord of the treasury from 1721 to 1742, is often spoken of as the earliest of English prime ministers, and in important respects he resembled prime ministers of later times. But the favor of the king was essential to the maintenance of his position, and he was dependent upon the influence of the crown, exerted in general elections and in preserving his parliamentary majority. Neither he nor Lord North, who was the principal minister of George III during the years 1770-1782, would allow himself to be called "prime minister." They insisted that there was no such office in the British constitution. The Younger William Pitt seems to have been the first to maintain that there ought to be a chief minister, recognized as such.

The long Ministry of the Younger Pitt no doubt did much to institutionalize the position of prime minister. He was the undisputed master of the cabinet and, from the general election of 1784 until his resignation in 1801, the unquestioned leader of the House of Commons. But in important respects his position differed from that of prime ministers in the Victorian age and in the twentieth century, most notably in the need which he recognized of the personal confidence and approval of the King. When he resigned in 1801, while still retaining his majority in the House, it was because the King refused to accept his policy of Catholic Emancipation. As late as 1839 Sir Robert Peel declined to form a ministry because the youthful Queen Victoria refused to give him a mark of confidence which he regarded as necessary, but this incident appears to have been the last of its kind.

The Ultimate Power of Decision. After the passage of the Reform Act of 1832, the ultimate power of decision in all important questions of governmental policy passed completely from the sovereign to the cabinet, whose members were responsible to the reformed House of Commons. This occurred only after the cabinet was able to dispense with the favor of the crown and rely solely on the House of Commons, backed by the new enlarged electorate. In the eighteenth and early nineteenth century before 1832, no ministry could survive without both the favor of the sovereign and the support of the House of Commons; but granted the former, the latter was normally forthcoming. The influence of the crown was lessened by legislation in the late eighteenth century, but it remained a potent force until the Reform Act, though near the end of this period there were a few occasions when the sovereign found it virtually impossible to resist ministerial pressure. Thus in 1829, George IV, against his personal wishes, agreed to an act admitting Catholics to parliament and to office; and during the crisis of the Reform Bill William IV yielded to his ministers in assenting to the creation of peers. In both cases, the unreformed House of Commons supported the ministry against the sovereign in passing legislation demanded by public opinion. Royal resistance was bound to be less effective under the new régime inaugurated by the Reform Act. For, in the words of a distinguished authority on modern English constitutional history, "The Reform Act of 1832 created for the first time an electorate which could not be controlled by the king and oligarchy, by whose cooperation the destinies of the country had been guided."

Persistence of Mixed Government. It was difficult for contemporaries to realize the character of the new constitutional system that had been created. Even Lord Melbourne, the Whig Prime Minister during most of the 1830's, suggested that it would be impossible to carry on the government without the rotten boroughs abolished by the Reform Act. The two great parties—Whigs and Tories—continued to uphold, even if with perhaps lessening conviction, the doctrine of mixed government. Lord Brougham, who had been Lord Chancellor in the Grey Ministry, in a book entitled *On Democracy and Mixed Monarchy,* written probably in 1843 or 1844, said: "The great virtue of the Constitution of England is the purity in which it recognizes and establishes the fundamental principle of all mixed governments; that the supreme power of the state being vested in several bodies, the consent of each is required to the performance of any legislative act. . . . The ruling powers are three—the Sovereign, the Lords, and the Commons."

Mixed Government Questioned. Yet there were men, including some political leaders, who realized that the Reform Act had affected constitutional relationships and that constitutional realities were no longer in harmony with the old and venerated theory of mixed government. Even Lord Brougham, in the book referred to, expressed the opinion that the case for mixed government rested upon the incapacity of the people for self-government, and that if this incapacity should come to an end, the argument for mixed government would fail. Sir Robert Peel, in a speech delivered in May, 1835, told his hearers that the government of the country "must, after all, be mainly conducted with the concurrence and through the immediate agency of the House of Commons." The group of men known as Colonial Reformers, who were active in the '30's and '40's of the nineteenth century, understood the principles of parliamentary government, with the ministers collectively responsible to the

House of Commons, and advocated the extension of this system to the more advanced of the British colonies. In 1844 there appeared in an English magazine a long article by a very influential member of this group, Edward Gibbon Wakefield, in which he anticipated by more than twenty years Bagehot's analysis of cabinet government based on the ascendancy of the House of Commons. (*See Reading No. 11.*)

Criticism of the House of Lords after 1832. There was considerable criticism of the House of Lords during the 1830's, after the passing of the Reform Act. This owed such strength as it had to existing political circumstances rather than to theoretical democratic objections to an aristocratic legislative body. But Philosophical Radicals, a name in use at this time for the followers of Bentham and the Utilitarian philosophy, were leaders in this criticism and in proposals for reform. The Whig (Liberal) Government, supported by a majority of the members of the reformed House of Commons, encountered difficulties in working the machinery of reformed mixed government with a large Tory (Conservative) majority in the House of Lords. In 1835 the Lords made drastic alterations in some important bills which had been passed by the House of Commons. In September of that year J. A. Roebuck, a Philosophical Radical, announced in the House of Commons his intention of presenting a motion in the next session of parliament to allow the Lords only a suspensive veto on bills bassed by the Commons. In an article published the following year, James Mill, the Scottish philosopher on whose shoulders the mantle of Bentham had fallen, proposed to exclude from the House of Lords the bishops of the Church of England, who had voted almost to a man against the Reform Bill and could be counted upon to oppose future reform measures in general, and Mill also proposed to leave the Lords only a suspensive veto on bills passed by the Commons, anticipating the Parliament Act of 1911. The tone of parliament being what it was at the time, such criticisms of the House of Lords as those of Roebuck and Mill could have no immediate effect.

The Referendal Theory. In the late 1830's a new theory was adumbrated which was to be invoked occasionally later in the nineteenth century and in the early years of the twentieth to justify the House of Lords in rejecting, on democratic grounds, a bill passed by the House of Commons. This "referendal theory," as it came to be called, was suggested by Lord John Russell in a speech in the House of Commons in 1839. He said that if an important bill, on which the House of Commons had been almost equally divided, were sent up to the House of Lords, the latter might properly say, "It appears that the Representatives of the people are very nearly evenly divided on the subject. We do not think that the country has made up its mind to this change. Let it be considered another year, and let us know whether it is a change called for by general opinion." In such a case the House of Lords would not be acting as a coordinate power in a system of mixed government, but as a guardian of democracy against a House of Commons that did not, or might not, express accurately the will of the people. Nearly twenty years later, in 1858, a bill to enable Jews to sit in parliament was debated in the House of Lords. (The effect of an act passed in the reign of William III requiring all members of parliament to abjure the Jacobite cause "on the true faith of a Christian" had been to exclude Jews from parliament.) The bill of 1858 was passed, and in the course of the debate in the House of Lords, Lord Lyndhurst took the position that it was the duty of the Lords to check the rash and ill-digested measures of the Commons, but that they ought not to block measures that were clearly supported by public opinion. (*See Reading No. 12.*)

Unsuccessful Reform Bills. The years 1832-1867 were almost barren of legislation in the field of major constitutional reform, apart from important reforms in local government, with which we are not concerned. In 1837 Lord John Russell, one of the authors of the Great Reform Bill, strongly opposed further parliamentary reform in a speech that earned for him the nickname of "Finality Jack." The "finality" of the Reform Act was abandoned in time, and in the 1850's reform bills were introduced in the House of Commons, but they did not result in legislation. The same was true of a bill in 1864 to extend the borough franchise, strongly supported by Gladstone. (*See Reading No. 13.*) The defeat of a later reform bill, in 1866, led to the resignation of the Min-

istry of Earl Russell (formerly Lord John), in which
Gladstone was leader of the House of Commons. In the
following year the Conservative Derby Ministry, in which
Disraeli was the leader of the House of Commons, carried through the Reform Act of 1867.

— 3 —

DEMOCRACY TRIUMPHANT, 1867-1914

The passage of reform acts in nineteenth-century Britain marked the transition from mixed government to
political democracy. Most of the adult male inhabitants
could vote before the century ended; and primarily because of the extensions of the suffrage, Britain could be
called a crowned republic when the First World War
broke out in the summer of 1914. The House of Commons was sensitive to the demands of the enlarged electorate, and the legislative power of the aristocratic House
of Lords had been limited by the Parliament Act of 1911.
The monarch then reigning, George V, has been hailed
as the model of a circumspect, constitutional king. Over
all, the cabinet was master; but it too was responsive to
public opinion outside parliament, as expressed in elections and in the press. The introduction of a wide franchise alone would not have sufficed to bring about political democracy, but in Britain other necessary conditions
were already present. Its people had long experience in
working representative institutions; the voter had a real
choice between the Liberal and the Conservative parties;
and he had access to the information needed to make an
intelligent choice. In short, the machinery of government existed by which the views of the enlarged electorate
could readily be translated into political action.

Parliamentary Reform Again. One of the main themes in British constitutional history in the years 1867-1914 is the broadening of the suffrage, by which political democracy evolved from what contemporaries had earlier united in calling a mixed government. Parliamentary reform became possible once more with the death in 1865 of Lord Palmerston, then Prime Minister, who had been strongly opposed to constitutional change after 1832. In 1866 the Liberal Government of Earl Russell tried to carry a reform bill that would have added about 400,000 voters to the electorate, but the more conservative Liberals in the House of Commons voted with the Conservatives to defeat the bill, the Russell Ministry resigned, and the Conservatives took office with Lord Derby as prime minister and Disraeli as leader of the House of Commons. This change of government produced a public agitation reminiscent of the May Days of 1832. Previously public apathy had been cited as an important reason for postponing parliamentary reform, but the issue came alive with all the suddenness of a flash flood. The lead was taken in London, where the so-called Hyde Park riots occurred. The working-class Reform League planned to hold a great meeting in Hyde Park, but at the last moment the Government denied the use of the park to the demonstrators. The crowd assembling for the meeting surged against the railings, which gave way in all directions, and broke into the park. This disturbance near the homes of the wealthier classes seems to have convinced them that electoral reform must not be delayed. Other evidence that delay might be dangerous was supplied by the open-air meetings organized by the democratic John Bright and the Reform League in London and other large cities.

The Reform Act of 1867. This powerful demand outside parliament for electoral reform helps to explain the nature of the Reform Act of 1867. The same House of Commons that had rejected the Liberal reform bill of 1866 now accepted from a Conservative Government a much more democratic measure; and the House of Lords, in contrast to its attitude in 1832, offered no resistance. The Reform Act of 1867 applied to England and Wales but not to Ireland and Scotland, for which reform acts, similar in principle but somewhat different in detail, were passed in 1868. The Act of 1867 added almost a million voters to the electorate in England and Wales. In terms of the increase in the size of the electorate, this was the most far-reaching of the nineteenth-century reform acts. (In 1832 the electorate was increased by about 50 percent; in 1867 by 88 percent; and in 1884 by 67 percent.) The principal beneficiaries were the urban workingmen in the boroughs. Since the Reform Act of 1867 discriminated in their favor as against the agricultural laborers in the counties, there could be no claim of "finality." A long step had been taken toward universal male suffrage, and it was only a question of time before the democratic tide would reach the countryside.

The Reform Bill of 1867, as originally introduced by Disraeli in the House of Commons, was much more conservative than the Bill as finally passed. In asking leave to introduce it, Disraeli explained that its aim was to strengthen the House of Commons by placing it on a more popular basis, but he distinguished between popular privileges and democratic rights, regarding the former, but not the latter, as consistent with a state of society in which there were great inequalities of condition. (*See Reading No. 14.*) Before the Bill was finally passed, the checks on democracy for which it provided had disappeared. The Reform Act extended the franchise in the boroughs to all householders who as owners or tenants had occupied dwelling houses within the boroughs for twelve months and paid the local taxes for the relief of the poor. The vote was also given to lodgers in the boroughs who had resided for twelve months as the only tenants in lodgings of a clear yearly value, unfurnished, of ten pounds or more a year. In the counties the qualification for copyholders and leaseholders was lowered from ten to five pounds, and the franchise was extended to occupiers of lands or tenements of a taxable value of twelve pounds or more a year. The Reform Act also provided for a redistribution of seats, though the changes that were made were much less sweeping than in 1832. Boroughs of less than 5,000 in population were disfranchised and those of less than 10,000 lost one seat each. Still another provision of the Reform Act rendered the life of parliament independent of that of the sovereign. The dissolution of parliament had followed automatically on the death of the sovereign until the passage of an act under William III provided that parliament should last for six months after a demise of the crown unless it was sooner dissolved by the new sovereign.

Growth of Party Organization. One clause in the Reform Act helped to produce a more complex party organization in Britain. Seats that had been lost by the small boroughs were distributed among the counties and the large towns. Where a three-member constituency was created, the voter was allowed to vote for only two members, the Conservatives hoping in this way to pick up a seat in Liberal constituencies. Their hopes were blighted in Birmingham, where a Liberal Association was formed to canvass the city ward by ward and instruct the voters how to cast their votes in the Liberal interest. In 1873 the Birmingham Liberal Association was reorganized by its secretary, Francis Schnadhorst, and by Joseph Chamberlain, who in his long and varied parliamentary career always received the city's support. Their Birmingham Plan was widely copied, and by 1877 a National Liberal Federation had been formed to assist in founding Liberal associations throughout the country. Meanwhile, the Conservatives had not been idle. As early as 1867 they had founded a National Union to woo the working-class vote, and three years later Disraeli organized the Conservative Central Office because he considered the older forms of organization "wholly insufficient . . . for an age of household suffrage and large popular constituencies." Thus, there dated from the Reform Act of 1867 an increasingly tighter party organization, and this shaped the workings of the British cabinet system in a striking fashion.

Gladstone's Great Ministry, 1868-1874. Despite Disraeli's hope of attaching many of the new voters to the Conservative party, it was the Liberals who were victorious in the general election of 1868, the first to be held after the passing of the Reform Act. Gladstone's first and greatest Ministry (1868-1874) was filled with a series of reforms. Some of these flowed from the Act of 1867, as, for example, an education act of 1870 that made possible a system of public elementary schools and the Ballot Act of 1872, providing for the use of the secret ballot in parliamentary elections. The purchase of army commissions was abolished, the universities were opened to Dissenters, competitive examinations were introduced throughout most of the civil service, and the judicial system was reorganized. As a result of the Judicature Act of 1873, and subsequent legislation, the national courts were organized as a "supreme court of judicature." This consisted of two branches: a high court of justice and a court of appeal. The former contained three divisions: chancery; king's bench (a consolidation of the old common-law courts); and probate, divorce, and admiralty. In almost all cases an appeal lay from the high court of justice to the court of appeal and thence to the House of Lords. By the Appellate Jurisdiction Act of 1876 the House of Lords was strengthened as a judicial body by provision for the appointment of two to four "lords of appeal in ordinary," who were virtually life peers. They were to be drawn from the occupants of high judicial office or from practising barristers in England and advocates in Scotland. By 1947 their number had been increased to nine. In the Act of 1876 the presence of three "lords of appeal" was declared necessary whenever an appeal was heard and determined by the House of Lords; and the Act designated as such the lord chancellor, those peers who had held high judicial office, and the "lords of appeal in ordinary," who were to be appointed under the Act.

The Reform Act of 1884. Gladstone's second Ministry (1880-1885) was marked by a further installment of parliamentary reform. The Reform Bill of 1884, giving the vote to the agricultural laborer in the counties on the same terms as it had been granted in 1867 to the town laborer, passed easily through the House of Commons. Since few politicians by this time were willing to oppose such a measure publicly, Gladstone scarcely bothered to justify it on principle. The real opposition came from the Conservative House of Lords, led by Lord Salisbury. Ever since 1832 the House of Lords—the majority of its members sitting by hereditary right—had often blocked important measures sent up from the House of Commons, either by amendment or rejection, whenever the Liberals had control of the House of Commons. Sir Ivor Jennings, a leading authority on the British constitution, has described the House of Lords as an outpost of the Conservative party. Its partisanship was clearly revealed in its acceptance from Conservative leaders of the more far-reaching Reform Bill of 1867 as contrasted with its recalcitrance in 1884. The Reform Bill of 1884 did not provide for a redistribution of seats; and on the ground that it should have done so, the House of Lords amended it and sent it back to the House of Commons. Invoking the referendal theory, Salisbury dared the Gladstone Government to take the quarrel to the voters for settlement. "If it is their judgment that there should be enfranchisement without redistribution," he said, "I should be very much surprised; but I should not attempt to dispute their decision."

Gladstone had no intention of allowing the House of Lords to bring about a general election at this time. Parliament was prorogued, and he prepared to send the Reform Bill to the Lords in an autumn session. Meanwhile the Radicals (a term applied to democratic Liberals) led a vigorous campaign against the House of Lords. John Bright proposed a plan that would have left the Lords only a suspensive veto, while Joseph Chamberlain and John Morley coined respectively the slogans "the peers against the people" and "mend them or end them." Alarmed at Radical vehemence, Queen Victoria arranged a conference between Gladstone and Salisbury, in which agreement was reached on a bill for the redistribution of seats. As a result the Lords passed the Reform Bill, and in the following year the Redistribution Bill became law.

Majorities Replace Communities. The Reform Act of 1884, which applied to the whole United Kingdom, assimilated the franchises in counties and boroughs. For the first time in English history the qualifications were the same in both types of constituencies. The household and lodger franchises were extended throughout the United Kingdom. Although some exceptions persisted, the effect of the Reform Act was to enfranchise almost the whole adult male population. By the Redistribution Act of 1885, on which Salisbury had insisted, twelve members were added to the House of Commons, making 670 in all. The principle of single-member constituencies was adopted, though twenty-seven constituencies were allowed two members each; and since 1885 the single-member constituency has predominated in the British electoral system. These constituencies were determined by population, and the old principle of the representation of communities yielded to the representation of majorities. While it is true that only a rough mathematical equality was achieved, it could be said that the Chartist ideal of equal electoral districts, each returning a single member, had virtually been realized. By comparison with what had been accomplished, there remained for settlement after 1885 only a few important issues in the field of electoral reform. These were woman suffrage, plural voting (by which some voters had extra votes), a closer approximation to equal electoral districts, and proportional representation for the purpose of giving minorities more adequate representation.

Public Opinion and the Government. One effect of parliamentary reform was to make both the cabinet and the House of Commons more sensitive to the trends of public opinion as reflected in elections, in the oratory of the pulpit and the platform, and in the press. After the Conservatives were defeated in the general election of 1868, Disraeli, who had succeeded Lord Derby as prime minister, resigned without waiting to meet the new parliament. That is to say, the ministry took its dismissal not from the House of Commons but from the electorate. This practice, which was in marked contrast to that of the years 1832-1867, has since been followed whenever general elections have gone decisively against the party in power. In 1874 Gladstone followed the Disraeli precedent, though with reluctance, protesting that it was the House of Commons, not the constituencies, that ought to dismiss the ministry.

Sometimes ministerial measures were attacked in the House of Commons on the ground that there had been no mandate for them from the electorate. This was the line taken by Lord Hartington, a conservative Liberal in the House of Commons, in expressing his opposition to the first Home Rule Bill for Ireland in 1886. Asserting that the power of the House of Commons was derived from the constituencies, he argued that the House had no "right to initiate legislation, especially immediately upon its first meeting, of which the constituencies were not informed." If this doctrine of the mandate were gen-

erally accepted, members of parliament would become
mere delegates of the constituencies, and not their representatives, an idea that had often been decried, notably
by Burke in his famous speech to the electors of Bristol.
These trends, reflecting the establishment of democracy,
were accelerated during the rest of the century.

The Cabinet and the House of Commons. The
growth of political democracy strengthened the cabinet
in dealing with the House of Commons and altered the
relationship between them. In the late nineteenth century, the majorities by which parties won general elections were usually so commanding that the cabinet had
little fear of losing control of the House. The mastery of
the cabinet was further strengthened by the growing in-
sistence of the constituencies that their representatives
carry out the party program and by the increasing dependence of the candidates on party machinery for election. To be elected in the enlarged constituencies, candidates needed the party label, and few would risk losing
it. That this trend has persisted can be seen from the fact
that in the election of 1951 every member of parliament
owed his election to the support of a party organization.
Since the expense of election was high and in the late
nineteenth century was still borne by the member himself, most members were unwilling to risk bringing on a
government defeat that might entail a general election.

In maintaining its control, the cabinet used whips, who
marshalled members of the House of Commons for the
necessary majorities. Speeches in the House ceased to
have an important influence on voting there, and it is
generally believed that their quality deteriorated. By the
end of the century, legislation was often carried through
without adequate scrutiny. Budgets received less attention. And the cabinet in order to expedite the conduct
of business resorted to time schedules and closure rules
to shut off debate. According to Sidney Low in his
thoughtful *Governance of England,* published in 1904,
"The House of Commons no longer controls the Executive; on the contrary, the Executive controls the House
of Commons." He also noticed that the House of Commons, which in the years 1832-1867 dismissed cabinets, no longer did so. "The real political sovereign, and
the arbiter of the destinies of cabinets," he declared, was

"the electoral body." Just as Bagehot's *English Constitution* contains illuminating insights into the workings of the British constitution in the years between the first and second reform bills, so Low's *Governance of England* is a penetrating and realistic description of how it operated in the early years of the twentieth century. (*See Reading No. 15.*)

Cabinet Size and Collectivism.   The cabinet, which at the beginning of the nineteenth century included about a dozen members, averaged about twenty on the eve of the First World War. This increase in membership was due mainly to the heightened governmental activity that followed the rise of a philosophy of more positive state action to improve social conditions, sometimes called collectivism, which has been defined as "the school of opinion . . . which favors the intervention of the State, even at some sacrifice of individual freedom, for the purpose of conferring benefit upon the mass of the people." In the late nineteenth century, if not earlier, collectivism had displaced the laissez-faire doctrines of the classical economists, who had held that enlightened self-interest, if given free scope, could be counted upon to promote the general welfare. Laissez-faire, a distinctly middle-class economic philosophy, was at its height when the middle classes were dominant in parliament, and it was to be expected that after 1867 it would be replaced by a philosophy more acceptable to the lower classes.

The Growth of Administration.   The factory legislation of the early nineteenth century marked a victory for collectivism over laissez-faire, and every triumph of collectivism has meant an increase in administration. New "boards," each with a president, were set up, including a board of works in 1851, a local government board in 1871, and a board of education in 1899. In such cases, the term "board" was a misnomer because no board was established. What was created was in effect an executive department, the president of the board being really a minister, who was usually a member of the cabinet. Changes had also taken place in older departments. The two secretaries of state of Elizabeth I had increased to five, namely, the secretaries of state for home affairs, foreign affairs, war, the colonies, and India. Of the other departments, that of the lord chancellor continued, somewhat changed, while the offices of lord president of the council and lord privy seal had long been sinecures. The old offices of lord high admiral and lord treasurer had long been in commission. The treasury was headed by a commission, consisting of the first lord and three junior lords; these were sinecure offices, the first of which was regularly held by the prime minister and the others by the whips of the party in office.

The Liberal Schism. The Liberal party, the main beneficiary at first of the broadened suffrage after 1867, entered a new phase after 1886. In that year Gladstone greatly weakened the party by insisting on Home Rule for Ireland at a time when imperialism was becoming very popular. There were desertions from two sides, first from the more conservative elements among the Liberals and then from the more radical. Lord Hartington led the more conservative Liberals in the House of Commons to the support of the Conservatives, while the defection of Liberal peers swelled the Conservative majority in the House of Lords. Before Gladstone introduced his Home Rule Bill, the Radical Joseph Chamberlain resigned from the Government. He and his followers joined the Hartington Liberals to defeat the Bill in the House of Commons; and subsequently the combined groups were known as Liberal Unionists, *i.e.,* Liberals who regarded Home Rule for Ireland as incompatible with the maintenance of the Union between Great Britain and Ireland which had been established in 1800. In 1895 they entered the Salisbury Government, which in consequence was known as a Unionist rather than a Conservative Government. As a result of the schism in the Liberal party, the Conservatives held office for two decades (1886-1905), except for a brief Liberal interlude from 1892 to 1895.

The Queen and Gladstone. Gladstone's conversion to Home Rule for Ireland also alienated Queen Victoria. Her dislike of Gladstone dated from the second administration of Disraeli (1874-1880), during which the latter had taught her to view Conservative foreign policy as her own. She never forgave Gladstone's severe criticism of that policy. She was highly critical of "the high-handed dictator style of Mr. Gladstone" that had produced the clash with the Lords in 1884; and the

breach became irreparable after he adopted the policy
of Home Rule, which she looked upon as threatening the
maintenance of her empire. In 1886 the Queen tried to
prevent Gladstone from taking office; and once he was
in, she intrigued to get him out. When it appeared that
he might ask for a dissolution, she consulted Salisbury,
then leader of the Opposition, to see whether one should
be granted. During Gladstone's fourth and last ministry
(1892-1894), she was coldly remote. No doubt she was
relieved, as apparently the majority of the British people
were, by the Lords' crushing rejection of Gladstone's
second Home Rule Bill in 1893 by a vote of 419 to 41.

The Monarchy after Queen Victoria. Despite repeated provocation, Gladstone remained discreetly silent.
The reign closed with the popularity of the monarchy
high. In 1887 and again in 1897 great jubilees were held
to celebrate Queen Victoria's long reign. She encouraged
her subjects during the Boer War (1899-1902); and the
publication of her letters after her death revealed to them
the assiduousness with which for over sixty years she
had attended to her duties. She was succeeded in 1901
by her son Edward VII, and he and his successors abandoned the ramparts to which she had clung so tena-
ciously. If Edward VII did not fully accept the implica-
tions of democracy, he was both more pliable and less
interested in politics than his predecessor. His successor,
George V, displayed sound judgment. During the passage
of the Parliament Act of 1911, despite strong personal
distaste for the measure, he cooperated with the Liberal
Government of Herbert Asquith in limiting the legislative power of the House of Lords.

The Liberals after 1906. On the whole the House
of Lords had contended successfully with the Gladston-
ian Liberals. It proved less fortunate in its dealings with
the revivified Liberal party that took office in 1905 after
the Conservative Prime Minister Arthur Balfour, a
nephew of Lord Salisbury, had resigned, following a
schism in the Conservative party over the tariff. In 1906
the Liberals won the greatest electoral victory in their
history, obtaining a majority in the House of Commons
of 82 over all other parties combined and of 219 over
the Conservatives. The height of collectivist legislation
before the First World War came during the years of

Liberal rule after 1906, when a series of reforms along collectivist lines was carried out with startling rapidity. Trade boards were set up to fix minimum wages, and an elaborate system of social insurance, modelled on German social legislation, brought the state into many spheres of activity formerly considered private. The Liberals were spurred on in this direction by the appearance of twenty-nine Labor members of parliament as a result of the election of 1906. They had been nominated by the Labor Representation Committee, which had taken shape in 1900. Its membership was drawn from the trade unions and such socialist bodies as the Fabian Society, the Social Democratic Federation, and the Independent Labor Party. (*See Reading No. 16.*) Although they could count on the support of twenty-four trade-union members among the Liberals, called "Lib-Labs," the Laborites were only a small minority before the war; and their views on many issues were similar to those of the Liberals.

The Liberals and the Lords. The House of Lords, quiescent during the years of Conservative (Unionist) rule from 1895 to 1905, bestirred itself early in the new régime. In 1906 it emasculated Liberal measures dealing with education, plural voting, and the liquor trade. In the following year, the Liberal Prime Minister, Sir Henry Campbell-Bannerman, presented a famous resolution to the effect that the legislative power of the House of Lords should be curbed so as to secure that, within the limits of a single parliament, the final decision of the House of Commons should prevail. In his supporting speech, he castigated as fantastic the claim of the Lords of a right to refer bills passed by the House of Commons to the country before they could become law. (*See Reading No. 17.*) This resolution had no immediate result, but it chalked out the future Liberal line in dealing with the House of Lords.

Rejection of the Finance Bill. Matters moved to a climax when the House of Lords in the fall of 1909 rejected the Lloyd George Finance Bill. New revenue was needed for naval rearmament and old age pensions; and David Lloyd George, the Chancellor of the Exchequer, proposed to raise it from more steeply graduated income and inheritance taxes, heavier duties on beer, spirits, and tobacco, and special taxes on land. It was this last proposal that aroused the peers, many of whom were great landowners. The proposed taxes on land included a heavy tax on the unearned increment of the land (the increase in its site value) and a tax on undeveloped land that would affect the holdings of the aristocracy. While the Finance Bill was still in the House of Commons, Lloyd George made a series of provocative speeches attacking individual peers by name. He had previously derided the House of Lords collectively as "Mr. Balfour's poodle," Balfour being at the time the Conservative leader in the House of Commons.

On November 23 Lord Lansdowne, the Conservative leader in the House of Lords, moved "That this House is not justified in giving its consent to this Bill until it has been submitted to the judgment of the country." A week later the Lords defeated the Finance Bill, claiming that it was not an ordinary revenue bill but a measure of social revolution. This was a serious action, for it left the government without revenue while challenging the generally accepted omnipotence of the House of Commons in money matters. Parliament was dissolved; and a general election was held in January, 1910, in which the Finance Bill and a limitation on the Lords' veto, as foreshadowed in the Campbell-Bannerman resolution, were prominent issues. The Liberals hoped for a clear mandate, but they failed to obtain it. Their majority over all other parties in the House of Commons disappeared, for they won only two more seats than the Conservatives and became dependent on the aid of Irish Nationalists and the Labor party. The Liberal Government, in which Asquith had succeeded Campbell-Bannerman as prime minister, remained in office; but it was henceforth a minority, not a majority, government. The Irish Nationalists and the Laborites were both interested, though for different reasons, in limiting the powers of the House of Lords; and on the other side, the Conservatives were stiffened in their devotion to the House of Lords by their recognition that its veto power was the last important barrier against Home Rule and sweeping social change.

The Parliament Bill.   On April 14, 1910, the Parliament Bill, which was framed on the lines of the Campbell-Bannerman resolution, was introduced in the House

of Commons. Two weeks later the Finance Bill passed
easily through both Houses. On May 6, Edward VII
died, and his son George V inherited the developing
crisis. After the breakdown of a constitutional conference, the Asquith Cabinet addressed a minute to the
King on November 15, advising a dissolution of parliament and a general election on the issue of the Lords'
veto. He was asked to agree to the creation of enough
peers to carry the Parliament Bill through the House
of Lords if the Liberals were successful in the election.
(*See Reading No. 18.*) The King assented, though with
reluctance. The general election of December, 1910—the
second in a year—wiped out the slim margin of superiority that the Liberals had possessed over the Conservatives, and they became more dependent than ever on
their allies. On February 11, 1911, Asquith again introduced the Parliament Bill, which went quickly through
the House of Commons. On July 24 an amended version
passed the House of Lords; but the Lords' amendments
were unacceptable to the Liberals, and the Asquith Government advised the King to create peers to end the
deadlock. A creation of fifty would have been enough
in 1832; over four hundred would have been needed in
1911. It appeared for a time that the House of Lords
would be swamped. "Die-Hard" peers led by Lord Hals-
bury conducted a "last-ditch" revolt against the more
moderate leadership of Lord Lansdowne, who had urged
the rejection of the Finance Bill but now favored acquiescence. On August 10, the day on which the House of
Lords would have to decide its course of action, the
Liberal Lord Morley read a communication from the
King to the effect that he would honor his pledge to create
peers; and when the division was taken, the Government
had won by 17 votes. Lansdowne and his followers re-
frained from voting; and the Government majority consisted of a combination of 80 Government supporters, 37
Conservative peers, and 13 bishops, including the two
archbishops.

The Parliament Act of 1911. The preamble to the
Parliament Act stated an intention of replacing the existing House of Lords with a second chamber resting on a
popular rather than an hereditary basis. This has never
been done, and it is an unreformed House of Lords that

exists in Britain today. Provision was made, however, for limiting the legislative power of the Lords. Under the terms of the Parliament Act, the House of Lords could delay a money bill for only one month. At the end of that time a money bill, if not passed without amendment, would become law without the consent of the Lords. The Act defined a money bill and provided that certification by the speaker of the House of Commons that a bill was a money bill should be decisive. Public bills other than money bills—except a bill to extend the maximum duration of parliament—would become law without the consent of the Lords if passed by the House of Commons in three successive sessions, whether of the same parliament or not, providing that an interval of two years should have elapsed. Before 1911 the maximum duration of parliament had been limited to seven years by the Septennial Act of 1716. A provision in the Parliament Act reduced the period to five years, which was applied to the existing parliament, and this could not be extended without the consent of the Lords. (*See Reading No. 19.*) The Parliament Act has been scarcely used, for only three acts have been passed under its terms. A Home Rule Bill for Ireland and a bill to disestablish the church in Wales were passed without the consent of the Lords in 1914, but their operation was suspended because of the war. And in 1949, a second Parliament Act, passed under the terms of the first, reduced the period of the Lords' power to delay legislation to one year.

It should be realized that the Parliament Act of 1911 did little more than put on a statutory basis the practice that had prevailed since 1832. The essence of the referendal theory, of which the Lords had made good use, was their claim of a right to delay legislation but not finally to reject it if the electorate supported it in a general election. On this latter point the new machinery obviated the need for a general election before an important bill could be passed after the Lords had rejected it. If the rules of the game had been somewhat rewritten to allow the Liberal party an opportunity to carry its program without resort to the electorate, still a two-year delay could be of consequence when the maximum duration of parliament was five years. That the Labor party, which after the First World War succeeded to the position that the Liberals had held earlier, did not consider the balance properly adjusted can be seen from the passage of the second Parliament Act in 1949. The Laborites had argued that they would have less time to carry out their legislative program, if the Lords should prove obstructive, than the Conservatives, who could count on having the full life of parliament.

Payment of Members of Parliament. In 1911 another important constitutional change occurred. Provision was made for the payment of members of parliament, a reform which had figured among the Six Points of the Chartist program. On the point of annual parliaments alone, that program has gone unfulfilled. The payment of members was a frank recognition that the end of an era had come in British politics. It could no longer be assumed that a member of parliament would have a private income and sufficient leisure to give his services to the state without compensation. On the eve of the First World War the wave of democracy that had been released by the Reform Act of 1867 had invaded the inner confines of what had once been considered the most exclusive gentlemen's club in Europe.

— 4 —

FROM DEMOCRACY TO SOCIALISM, 1914-1956

On August 4, 1914, Britain entered the First World War, and for four years the British people lived in a state of national emergency. When it ended, in 1918, an exhausted nation faced the future with a heavy debt, declining foreign trade, and, after 1921, serious unemployment in basic industries. Despite these handicaps, social services were expanded; and after the onset of the depression in 1929, the government distributed relief from public funds to those of the unemployed who were covered by law. But the welfare state was incomplete until the advent in 1945 of the Attlee Labor Government which may be said to have socialized Britain. In the arduous years between the wars (1919-1939), British parliamentary democracy proved relatively stable, but anti-democratic ideologies triumphed in Russia, Italy and Germany; and democracy, which before 1914 had come to seem almost the badge of civilization, was placed on the defensive.

Under these circumstances, the British constitution underwent modification. But it is noteworthy that those of its features that had engaged Sidney Low's attention at the beginning of the century still seemed characteristic of it to observers fifty years later. There had been a strengthening of the tendencies already in existence when Low wrote, but there had been no sharp break with the past. The emergencies of war and depression accelerated trends already in motion. As the twentieth century unrolled, the cabinet continued to gain power at the expense of the House of Commons, democracy continued to grow, and the social philosophy of collectivism scored new triumphs. A constitutional history of these years will have to consider the cabinet in peace and war, electoral reform and party fortunes, the growth of administration that accompanied the rise of collectivism, and the legislation which reflected the twin influences of democracy and collectivism.

Wartime Conditions.   Despite prewar internal controversies, the people of Britain were united when they entered the First World War. Asquith, who remained Liberal prime minister until December, 1916, announced that controversial legislation would be suspended. Party differences were put aside, and his Liberal Cabinet became a Coalition Cabinet in 1915, when representatives of the Conservative and Labor parties joined it. To avoid the partisan acrimony of a general election in wartime, the life of the existing parliament, which had begun in 1910, was extended by its own act, and it was not finally dissolved until November, 1918. This power of parliament to prolong its own duration is a striking example of parliamentary sovereignty and of the flexibility of the British constitution. The House of Commons lost its remaining legislative initiative for the duration of the conflict and became in effect little more than a rubber stamp for government measures. Under the Defense of the Realm Act of 1914, popularly known as DORA, the government was empowered to issue regulations for securing public safety and the national defense, and subsequent acts defined and added to this sweeping grant of authority. (*See Reading No. 20.*) Breach of the regulations could lead to court martial, and in the interests of national security the government intervened in many seemingly unrelated matters. Some regulations were questioned during the war, but the effect of Rex *v.* Halliday, a case decided by the House of Lords in 1917, was virtually to rule out court interference with the exercise of the legislative powers delegated to the government by the Defense of the Realm Act.

Conduct of the War. The foresightedness of prewar planning enabled Britain to move with comparative ease to a war footing; but after this phase passed, influential newspapers began to argue that the peacetime cabinet was inadequate to cope with the conditions of modern war. In an effort to achieve greater efficiency and flexibility, the Asquith Government made extensive use of committees, chief of which was a War Committee that possessed a secretariat. When the War Committee itself became unwieldy, *The Times,* which wanted Lloyd George as prime minister in place of Asquith, urged that a change would have to be made. In December, 1916, in a move that split the Liberal party badly, Lloyd George notified Asquith that he would resign unless the War Committee was limited to four members, of whom the Prime Minister would not be one. Asquith refused, and Lloyd George resigned. A few days later Asquith followed suit; and when the Conservative leader A. Bonar Law declined to form a government, Lloyd George took office. It is noteworthy that the House of Commons played no part in this ministerial crisis. It had nothing to do with making Lloyd George prime minister.

The War Cabinet. Composed originally of only five members, the Lloyd George War Cabinet inherited

the secretariat of the War Committee and the far-reaching
authority of the cabinet. Like the Asquith Cabinet which
it superseded, the War Cabinet was a coalition, with the
Liberal Lloyd George as prime minister, the Conservative[1] Lord Curzon as lord president of the council, the
Conservative Bonar Law as chancellor of the exchequer,
and the Conservative Lord Milner and the Laborite
Arthur Henderson as ministers without portfolio, meaning thereby members of the cabinet who were not heads
of departments. The complexion of the Cabinet was
predominantly Conservative. With the exception of
Bonar Law, its members were free from departmental
duties, a complete departure from the practice of the
peacetime cabinet. The functions of administration and
policy-making were deliberately separated; and most of
the members of the War Cabinet were enabled to give
their attention to policy-making and the coordination of
the departments. Moreover, except for Bonar Law they
scarcely attended parliament. Its small size, the freedom
of its members from administrative duties, and its efficient methods of conducting business were the chief
characteristics of the Lloyd George War Cabinet. The
complete secrecy of cabinet proceedings came to an end.
In its first year the War Cabinet had about 250 visitors,
including experts in various branches of administration.
The climax came with the publication of War Cabinet
Reports in 1917 and 1918 that explained what had occurred and how the War Cabinet conducted its business.
(*See Reading No. 21.*) This was a startling divergence
from the practice of earlier cabinets, an account of which
was given by Lord Curzon in the House of Lords in
June, 1918. (*See Reading No. 22.*)

[1] Strictly speaking, Curzon and the others here called Conservatives were Unionists. Late in the nineteenth century, most of the Liberal Unionists united with the
Conservatives to form a Unionist party in a common
opposition to Gladstone's policy of Home Rule for Ireland, which they saw as threatening the Union between
Great Britain and Ireland. But after 1922, when most
of Ireland was organized as the Irish Free State, the
term Unionist lost its meaning; and the name Conservative party was used once more. For the sake of continu-
ity, the term Conservative is used throughout this book.

The End of the War Cabinet. The War Cabinet continued for a short time after the war. Following the so-called Khaki Election of December, 1918, which went heavily in favor of the Lloyd George Coalition, a new War Cabinet was formed. The House of Commons unexpectedly asserted itself in October, 1919, by defeating a Government measure, and a few days later it was announced that the small War Cabinet had been given up. A new cabinet of twenty members, including the heads of the great departments, took its place. In the interwar period, the cabinet usually included about twenty members. Important innovations of the War Cabinet, however, persisted. The secretariat was continued, and the extreme secrecy of prewar cabinets was not revived. After 1919 the cabinet met more frequently than before the war and made more use of committees.

Electoral Reform. Another important outgrowth of the war was electoral reform. The Representation of the People Act of 1918, which became law in February of that year, was in some respects more radical than any previous reform act. It more than doubled the electorate, provided a new basis for manhood suffrage, gave the vote to women, though not on the same terms as to men, limited plural voting, introduced the principle of proportional representation, though on a very limited basis, and replaced by a single statute the tangle of legislation in which electoral law had formerly to be sought. Like the acts of 1832 and 1867, it provided both for extension of the parliamentary franchise and a redistribution of seats.

The Franchise. As regards the franchise, the Act of 1918 abolished the previous property qualifications, and no longer was any relationship to property required for voting. Henceforth, a man could vote in the constituency in which he had registered if, at the time of registration, he had reached the age of twenty-one and had resided for at least six months in the constituency, or had occupied therein business premises of the annual value of ten pounds or more for the same period. A number of the British universities were also parliamentary constituencies, and in these a man could vote, subject to the same age requirement, if at the time of registration he held a degree from the university. However, he could have at the most only two votes, the maximum number for any voter after 1918. University representation in parliament had begun in the early seventeenth century, when James I gave the status of parliamentary constituencies to the universities of Oxford and Cambridge. The same status was given to Trinity College, Dublin, by the Act of Union of 1800, and to the University of London and four Scottish universities (grouped to form two constituencies) by the Reform Act of 1867. The Act of 1918 raised the number of university members to a total of fifteen and also provided that in university constituencies a method of proportional representation should be used if two or more members were to be elected. It has been estimated that the Act of 1918 added about two million men to the electorate.

Woman suffrage had been advocated at the time of the Chartist movement. The agitation for it grew rapidly in the early years of the twentieth century, but the tactics of the militant "suffragettes," who resorted to various forms of violence to accomplish their objective, outraged public opinion. Upon the outbreak of the war in 1914, however, the militants patriotically declared a truce; and during the war it came to be generally felt that British women, by virtue of their war services and sacrifices, had earned the right to vote. Under the Act of 1918 a woman could vote if at the time of registration she had reached the age of thirty and was entitled to be registered as a local government elector or was the wife of a man so entitled. Women were also permitted to vote in university constituencies subject to the same age requirement. It has been estimated that some six million women were added to the electorate in 1918. They were not given the vote on the same terms as men because women were more numerous than men in the population, and parliament was not prepared to give them a preponderance in the electorate. It was not until 1928, when the Equal Franchise Act was passed, that women received the vote on the same terms as men. (*See Reading No. 23.*) Another act of 1918 admitted women to the House of Commons, but it was decided in 1922 that a woman could not sit in the House of Lords.

Redistribution of Seats. The redistribution of seats provided for in the Act of 1918 increased the membership of the House of Commons from 670 to 707, which latter figure was reduced to 615 when the Irish Free State was organized in 1922. The principle of the single-member constituency, which had been generally adopted in 1885, was continued, though a few constituencies were given two members each and one was given three. The ratio of representation to population was approximately 1 to 70,000, except in Ireland, where it was approximately 1 to 43,000. One result of the system of single-member constituencies, in which whoever gets the largest number of votes, whether a majority or not, wins, was that the percentage of seats won by a party has often borne little relation to its percentage of the popular vote. The Liberal party, which became a permanent minority party in the years after the First World War, suffered most from this system and was foremost in advocating the adoption of some kind of proportional representation. So far it has had no success.

The Parties between the Wars. Between 1900 and 1935 the electorate was more than quadrupled. In the former year there were less than seven million voters in Britain; in the latter there were almost thirty million, though the greater part of Ireland was no longer in the United Kingdom. With this enlargement of the electorate went changes in the parties. In the interwar years the Conservatives were generally dominant, the Labor party was the official opposition, and the Liberals were in decline. Except for the years 1929-1931, the Conservative party was the strongest in the House of Commons, and in 1931 it won the largest majority in British parliamentary history. The Conservative ascendancy lasted until the close of the Second World War in 1945. In the interwar years the chief Conservative leaders were, successively, Bonar Law, Stanley Baldwin, and Neville Chamberlain (a son of Joseph Chamberlain). Bonar Law became prime minister in 1922 after the breakup of the Lloyd George Coalition; and when he resigned in May, 1923, he was succeeded by Stanley Baldwin, despite the greater reputation of Lord Curzon. Since the strength of the Labor party was concentrated in the House of Commons, it was thought necessary that the prime minister should be a member of that House. In fact, no prime minister has sat in the House of Lords since Lord Salisbury resigned in 1902; and the rule that the prime minister must be a member of the House of Commons has become a recognized convention of the constitution. Baldwin was succeeded in 1937 by Neville Chamberlain, who was prime minister when Britain entered the Second World War in 1939.

In these years the Labor party became a major party in place of the Liberals, who never recovered from the split of December, 1916, when they had been compelled to choose between Asquith and Lloyd George. Before 1914 the Labor party was a small minority party, never electing more than fifty members to the House of Commons, but in 1918 it adopted a new constitution that strengthened it greatly. For the first time membership was thrown open to individuals, who could now join the party without belonging first to a trade union or a socialist society. The Labor party also adopted a new program calling for the nationalization of major industries, but it did not possess sufficient strength in parliament to carry through a socialist program until 1945. Before that it held office twice, in 1924 and again from 1929 to 1931, but it was dependent at both times on Liberal support.

The Crisis of 1931. The second Labor Government, in which J. Ramsay MacDonald was prime minister, came to an end in circumstances that badly hurt the Labor party. It took office just as the great depression was beginning, and by the summer of 1931 unemployment had reached almost three million. In August, while Parliament was not in session, the MacDonald Government was faced with a financial emergency. The economic situation had become so unfavorable that a large foreign loan was necessary to save the gold standard; and to reassure foreign investors, the budget for the coming year had to be balanced. Heavier taxes and economies in government were necessary. MacDonald became convinced that a 10 percent reduction in the unemployment benefit, popularly called the dole, would have to be made, despite the opposition of the Trades Union Congress, of many influential members of his Cabinet, and of the overwhelming majority of his followers in parliament. In the evening of August 23 the Cabinet authorized him to tender to the King the resignation of the Ministry, the assumption being that Baldwin, as leader of the Conservative party, would be asked to form a new ministry to carry through the needed economies.

Formation of the National Government. It was not, however, a Conservative Government with Baldwin as prime minister that emerged, but a so-called National Government, virtually a coalition, with MacDonald as prime minister. King George V had been informed earlier of the rift in the Labor Cabinet and had decided to consult the Opposition leaders. Baldwin could not be reached, and he saw first the Liberal Sir Herbert Samuel, who advised him to retain MacDonald as prime minister, if possible with a Labor cabinet, if not with a cabinet composed of members of the three parties, Labor, Conservative, and Liberal. When MacDonald arrived at Buckingham Palace in the evening of August 23 to tender the resignation of the Labor Ministry, the King, according to the account given by his private secretary, told him that he was the only man to lead the country through the crisis. On the following morning, the Prime Minister reached an understanding with Baldwin and Samuel as to the formation of a National Government. Later that day he tendered the resignation of the Labor Government and accepted the King's commission to form a National Government with himself as prime minister. The new Cabinet consisted of only ten members —MacDonald and three of his Labor colleagues, four Conservatives, and two Liberals. Soon afterward MacDonald was deposed from the Labor party leadership, and he and his followers were expelled from the party. The National Government was not so comprehensive as its name implied. It was really a coalition of Conservatives, Liberals, and a small minority of Laborites who called themselves the National Labor party. The great majority of the Labor party were in opposition to it.

The crisis of 1931 is memorable for a number of reasons. As leader of the Labor party, MacDonald's course in not consulting his Labor colleagues about the formation of a National Government was extraordinary; and after he accepted the King's commission to form such a government, he ceased to be the leader of the Labor party. Yet the premiership had long been bound up with party leadership; and as prime minister without being head of a party he occupied an anomalous position. There is some reason for concluding that he owed it to the will of the King and the willingness of the Conservatives and Liberals to support him. There have been varied estimates of the role of George V in this crisis. Sidney Webb and Harold Laski, both members of the Labor party, reached diametrically opposed conclusions. Webb contended that the King had acted with strict constitutional propriety; Laski thought that the National Government was the result of a "palace revolution."

The Agreement to Disagree. In the interest of economy, the National Government was given extraordinary powers by parliament, including the power to reduce authorized appropriations, but a few months later Britain went off the gold standard, which this Government had been formed to maintain. In October, 1931, there was a general election, in which the National Government asked for and obtained a "doctor's mandate" to cure the economic malady, but it was not in agreement as to the remedies to be prescribed. The Conservatives advocated a protective tariff, to which the Liberals were strenuously opposed; and MacDonald insisted on freedom to consider every proposal. The National Government won a smashing victory, obtaining nine-tenths of the seats in the House of Commons, while the Labor party for the time being was submerged. Voting strength in the new House of Commons lay with the Conservatives, who had won 470 seats, and their overwhelming strength portended protectionist legislation. When comprehensive and permanent tariff measures were foreshadowed, the Liberals and the Laborite Lord Snowden prepared to resign from the cabinet but were persuaded to remain with the understanding that they were free to oppose by speech and vote the protectionist measures advocated by the majority of the Cabinet. This agreement to disagree ran counter to the principle of collective responsibility which had long been considered a distinguishing characteristic of the British cabinet system, and no parallel to it can be found in modern British constitutional practice. It did not pass unchallenged, though the resolutions of censure that were introduced in both Houses were easily defeated. "Mr. MacDonald," commented the *Manchester*

Guardian, "has in six months been the instrument for carrying through two constitutional revolutions. In the autumn he broke up the British party system. Last week he broke up the Cabinet system."

Abdication of Edward VIII. In 1936 there occurred an event without precedent in British history—the voluntary abdication of a sovereign. In January, 1936, George V died and was succeeded by his eldest son, the Prince of Wales, as Edward VIII. In the summer and late autumn of that year the new King's attentions to Mrs. Wallis Warfield Simpson received publicity in the United States in newspapers that were widely read in Canada and, to some extent, in Britain. Mrs. Simpson was of American birth but had become a British subject as the result of a second marriage, contracted after she had obtained a divorce from her first husband in an American court. In October, 1936, she started proceedings for a divorce from her second husband in a British court, which granted her petition. Gossip was rife in London, and Baldwin, who had succeeded MacDonald as prime minister in the previous year, became concerned about the possible injury that might be done to the monarchy. He intimated to the King that British public opinion would not sanction his marriage to Mrs. Simpson. Late in November the King asked him whether he thought that a morganatic marriage would be possible, and Baldwin, at the King's request, put this question to the Cabinet and the governments of the British Dominions. The responses were adverse, and the Prime Minister felt obliged to make it clear to the King that he must choose between marriage to Mrs. Simpson and the throne. On December 10 the King, who had already indicated to the Prime Minister his determination to marry Mrs. Simpson, executed an instrument in the form of a Declaration of Abdication, which was a personal act, performed without ministerial advice or responsibility. (*See Reading No. 24.*) The Declaration was given legal effect by an act which was hurried through parliament and received the King's assent on the following day. In accordance with its provisions, his brother, the Duke of York, succeeded to the throne as George VI.

The Growth of Administration. A subject in British constitutional history comparable in importance to the rise of political democracy is the growth of administration, though it has received less attention. The triumph of collectivism brought with it an expansion of governmental functions, which added greatly to the number of civil servants needed to perform them. The conditions of modern war also led to a marked increase of governmental activity, which took place both during and after the two world wars of this century. New executive departments were established, and the older departments grew larger and more complex. The government was also active in business, notably through the post office, which for many years has carried on the telegraph and telephone business and maintained savings banks. Little wonder that the number of civil servants in 1949 reached 706,197 exclusive of some 400,000 industrial workers (employed in ordnance factories, arsenals, dockyards, etc.).

Reform of the Civil Service. Fortunately, long before the growth of administration had reached these mammoth proportions, the civil service was reformed and high standards of efficiency imposed. The famous Northcote-Trevelyan Report of 1853 recommended open competitive examinations as the means of recruiting the civil service and proposed the establishment of a central examining board. Two years later the Civil Service Commission was set up to examine all persons nominated for appointment to junior positions in the civil service, but open competition did not become compulsory throughout most of the civil service until 1870. The examinations have recognized the distinction between intellectual and routine work, and those for the higher administrative posts have reflected the classical and mathematical learning of Oxford and Cambridge. The honor graduates of these universities have been the most successful candidates.

The Civil Service. Civil servants have been defined as "those servants of the Crown, other than holders of political or judicial offices, who are employed in a civil capacity, and whose remuneration is paid wholly and directly out of monies voted by Parliament." Among the officeholders excluded by this definition are the ministers, who are the political heads of departments and are responsible to parliament for the conduct of administration,

and their parliamentary secretaries—or parliamentary
under-secretaries, as they are called in departments headed
by secretaries of state—who usually sit in a different
house of parliament from the ministers. Included within
the terms of the definition are the highly efficient permanent secretaries, who play no part in politics but direct
a host of lesser officials descending to charwomen and
porters, whose tasks are routine and require little train-
ing. Those in the higher ranges of the civil service, who
form the administrative class, are responsible for much
more than the routine administration of the laws. They
study policies, frame legislative projects to make administration more efficient, and generally form the pivot
of the civil service. In 1949 the administrative class
numbered 4,316, a fraction of one percent of the whole.

Delegated Legislation. With the growth of administration has come the development of administrative
legislation (usually spoken of as delegated legislation)
and administrative justice. The term *delegated legislation*
refers to the practice by which parliament has delegated
legislative power, not excluding the power of taxation,
to ministers, departments, and other authorities. Delegated
legislation was uncommon until the middle of the nineteenth century, but since then it has grown greatly as the
functions of the central government have expanded. Parliament, unable to legislate in detail on all subjects, has
delegated power to subordinate authorities, enabling them
to issue orders, rules, and regulations. The annual output
of these has long exceeded in bulk that of parliamentary
legislation. Moreover, unlike parliamentary legislation,
which cannot be legally limited, delegated legislation is
limited by the terms of the delegating statute. Courts
have sometimes pronounced regulations *ultra vires*, that
is, beyond the legal power of the authority that issued
them.

The New Despotism? Although there is general
agreement that delegated legislation is necessary, there
has been serious criticism of its defects, which are attributable, in part at least, to its haphazard and unsystematic
development. Among the leading critics was Lord Chief
Justice Hewart, who in his *New Despotism*, published in
1929, charged that there was a deliberate attempt within
the civil service to place government departments above

parliament and beyond the range of the courts. In that year a committee was appointed to investigate the legislative and judicial powers exercised by ministers under statutory authority. This Committee on Ministers' Powers, in its report published in 1932, found no evidence of conspiracy within the civil service. But it distinguished between what it called normal and exceptional delegations of power and raised questions about the latter. In the normal type of delegated legislation, the Committee pointed out, limits were defined and could be enforced in the courts. The authority to which power was delegated was not empowered to legislate on matters of principle or to impose taxes or to amend acts of parliament. Occasionally, however, exceptional delegations of power had occurred. For example, the Import Duties Act of 1932 had empowered the treasury to levy additional duties on the recommendation of an advisory committee. A few acts of parliament had authorized subordinate authorities to modify the provisions of statutes. Sometimes acts had provided that regulations should have effect as if they were included in the acts themselves, apparently in order to prevent the courts from inquiring into the legal validity of the regulations. And other acts had provided that the making of regulations under the acts should be "conclusive evidence" that the requirements of the acts had been met. These attempts to exclude judicial review under the *ultra vires* principle were condemned by the Committee and since 1932 have generally been abandoned.

Safeguards against Abuses. Before the Second World War, there were four principal means of guarding against abuses of delegated legislation, but no one of these was satisfactory by itself, and taken together they did not form a systematic and comprehensive set of safeguards. They were: judicial review; the provisions for parliamentary control found in statutes that delegated legislative power; the provision for publicity found in the Rules Publication Act of 1893; and the doctrine that a minister was responsible to parliament for the activity of his subordinates. It has been seen that judicial control was sometimes evaded because of the way in which statutes were drafted. Sometimes statutes which authorized the making of regulations stipulated that they must be laid before parliament, but no consistent rule was adopted to govern the conditions under which this should be done. The Rules Publication Act of 1893 provided for the publication of the more important classes of delegated legislation both before and after they had been enacted. But there were many regulations which did not come within the scope of the Act. So far as the doctrine of ministerial responsibility was concerned, it had become increasingly difficult to hold a minister responsible to parliament under the modern cabinet system. When Lloyd George was asked by the Committee on Ministers' Powers whether he wished to make the control of parliament more effective, he replied: "Well, it has not got control. . . . Parliament really has no control over the Executive; it is a pure fiction."

Select Committee on Statutory Instruments. The Committee on Ministers' Powers recommended among other things that a standing committee of each house of parliament should be appointed at the beginning of each session to report on every bill delegating legislative powers and on all regulations made under delegating statutes. For over a decade it appeared that this part of the report would pass into oblivion, though delegated legislation continued to increase in volume. The issue was raised dramatically in January, 1937, by the Liberal member of parliament, Dingle Foot (*see Reading No. 25*), but he spoke to an almost empty House of Commons. When Britain entered the Second World War, the flow of regulations reached flood proportions. In 1944 a Select Committee on Statutory Instruments was established for the purpose of determining whether rules and orders laid before the House of Commons contained objectionable features, and since about 70 percent of all rules and orders go before the House, the scope of the Committee's work is wide. In 1946 the Rules Publication Act of 1893 was repealed by an act that also provided for a uniform procedure in numbering, printing, publishing, and citing rules and orders.

Administrative Justice. Like administrative (or delegated) legislation, administrative justice has grown up unsystematically and has been the subject of critical attention. The term refers to the judicial powers which parliament has granted to ministers, executive departments, and official tribunals, outside the regular judicial system, that affect the rights and property of citizens and corporate bodies. Beginning about 1870 statutes have occasionally given to ministers and departments and official bodies connected with departments the power to decide cases in dispute between administrative authorities and other parties and have sometimes provided that these decisions should be final, without appeal to the regular law courts. The authorities in which judicial powers have been vested are commonly called "administrative tribunals," and this term is used to include all judicial authorities which do not conform to normal English judicial standards. Not very much is known about the procedure of administrative tribunals. Their proceedings are private, and most of them do not give reasons for their decisions or publish reports of cases. In the Board of Education v. Rice, a case that came before the House of Lords on appeal in 1911, it was held that the Board, an executive department, in deciding a dispute need not conform in its procedure to a court of law, although it was stated that it must act fairly. The standards of administrative tribunals are very different from those prevailing in the law courts. In the latter, the judges must be trained in law and not subject to pressure or influence; both parties must be heard; proceedings must be public; evidence must be given in open court; witnesses must be subject to cross-examination; and the person giving the decision must be known. That administrative tribunals were not bound by these standards was made even more explicit in the well-known case of Local Government Board v. Arlidge (1915), in which Lord Haldane gave the decision for the House of Lords. Administrative justice is generally conceded to need reform, but very little has been accomplished in this direction.

Wartime Again.   The German armies attacked Poland on September 1, 1939, and two days later Britain was at war once more. The pattern set in the First World War was repeated with variations. An electoral truce was arranged among the parties by which it was agreed that seats would not be contested in by-elections, while annual acts for prolonging the life of parliament postponed the general election that would have normally taken place in 1940 until July, 1945, after the defeat of Germany. The Labor and Liberal parties gave support to Neville Chamberlain's Conservative Government, though they did not enter the Government until Winston Churchill (who had been first a Conservative, then a Liberal, and was now a Conservative again) became prime minister in May, 1940. The important acts that provided for emergency executive action were the Emergency Powers (Defense) Acts of 1939 and 1940. (*See Reading No. 26.*) The defense regulation that attracted the most attention was Regulation 18B, which authorized the home secretary to detain persons if he believed it necessary. In Liversidge *v.* Anderson, the House of Lords decided in 1942 that the minister's decision was not subject to judicial review (*see Reading No. 27*), and this made it impossible for anyone thus detained to secure redress no matter how much he might have been wronged.

The War Cabinets. It was assumed after the First World War that if Britain went to war again the cabinet would be remodelled along the lines of the Lloyd George War Cabinet. In fact, however, neither Chamberlain nor Churchill followed exactly the Lloyd George pattern, and their war cabinets can better be described as a compromise between the First World War Cabinet and the normal peacetime cabinet. The Chamberlain War Cabinet contained nine members, five of whom had heavy administrative duties. In his first few months as prime minister, Churchill experimented with a cabinet of five members, without administrative duties, who served as chairmen of committees, of which the department heads were members. By January, 1941, the cabinet had eight members, the majority of whom had administrative duties. In his *Gathering Storm* (1948), Churchill explained why he preferred a cabinet composed of heads of departments. (*See Reading No. 28.*) While the War Cabinet in principle retained control, the war was conducted on the military side by Churchill as defense minister (without a department) and on the civilian side by Sir John Anderson, who was lord president of the council and chairman of a very active committee. In February, 1942, Churchill, speaking in the House of Commons, described the importance of this committee: "The Lord President of the Council presides over what is, in certain respects, almost a parallel Cabinet concerned with home affairs. . . . An immense mass of business is discharged at their frequent meetings, and it is only in the case of a serious difference or in very large questions that the War Cabinet as such is concerned."

Wartime Innovations. There were a number of wartime innovations, among them the designation of Clement Attlee, the leader of the Labor party, as deputy prime minister. More permanent was the office of minister of state, first created in 1940 for war purposes. After October, 1943, a minister of state became an assistant to the secretary of state for foreign affairs because of the heavy administrative burdens in the Foreign Office. He enjoyed, nevertheless, full ministerial rank. His position was superior to that of the parliamentary under-secretary, and important matters were referred to him for decision. On difficult problems he consulted the secretary of state, who was responsible to the House of Commons for the conduct of the department. In the Conservative Government of Sir Anthony Eden in 1956 there were five ministers of state: two in the Foreign Office, and one each in the Colonial Office, the Scottish Office, and the Board of Trade. They were not in the cabinet, but they were members of the ministry and of parliament, most of them sitting in the House of Commons.

New Departments and Their Effects. A noticeable effect of the Second World War was an increase in the number of departments. After 1939 six permanent departments were created: the ministry of food (1939), of supply (1939), of fuel and power (1942), of town and country planning (1943), of national insurance (1944), and of civil aviation (1944). This was the greatest increase of permanent departments that ever took place within so short a time in British history, and some of its effects were noteworthy. There has been a stronger tendency than earlier toward a hierarchy of ministers because since 1945 there have been a dozen or more ministers, heads of major departments, who could not be included in the cabinet without making it unwieldy. A marked trend has also developed toward establishing standing committees of the cabinet, of which the excluded ministers have been members. Committees of the cabinet for temporary purposes have a long history, but a system of permanent cabinet committees has appeared since the Second World War. As has been recently remarked, "there are reasons for believing that a system of standing Cabinet committees is now well accepted and that indeed a formal pattern is beginning to emerge." The actual pattern of these standing committees will be determined by the prime minister at a given moment, and no chart of the committee structure is available since its publication would destroy the privacy that still shrouds cabinet proceedings.

The Postwar Labor Government. In the general election of July, 1945, held after the surrender of Germany, the Labor party won a majority of 146 seats over all other parties; and under the leadership of Attlee, it put into effect the socialist program to which it had been pledged for a generation. In its election manifesto, the Labor party had promised to ensure full employment and high production by maintaining purchasing power through good wages, social services, and taxation that would bear less heavily on low-income groups. In its first three years, the Attlee Government provided social security, including a national health service, from the cradle to the grave; and during the Labor régime, the following basic industries were nationalized: the Bank of England and civil aviation in 1946; coal and telecommunications in 1947; inland transport and electricity in 1948; gas in 1949; and iron and steel in 1951. Private ownership disappeared in these industries, and they became government monopolies.

The New Public Boards. To control the nationalized industries, the Attlee Government established public boards or corporations, composed of representatives of management and labor, entirely outside the civil service, and responsible through ministers to parliament and ultimately to the public. The use of independent bodies was not new, for there were well over a hundred authorities of different types free from the day-to-day control of ministers. What was unusual was the attempt to graft ministerial control onto a system of public boards (Coal Board, Transport Commission, etc.), which had so much power and responsibility because of their control of major industries. To secure ministerial responsibility without stifling the freedom of action required by the boards has been a continuing problem. (*See Reading No. 29.*) In general the relationship between the responsible minister and the central board has followed this pattern: The minister has been given the responsibility for framing general policy, while the board has the responsibility for day-to-day administration, including the employing and dismissal of the higher executives. The difficulties encountered by the House of Commons in obtaining information about the nationalized industries under these arrangements led to the appointment of a select committee during the 1954-1955 session to examine their reports and accounts and to report to the House, within clearly defined limits, on their current policies and practices.

The Second Parliament Act.   The Labor party had given notice that it would not tolerate obstruction by the House of Lords; and in the fall of 1947 the Attlee Government introduced a bill that became the Parliament Act of 1949. This provided that a bill would become law if it passed the House of Commons in two successive sessions, provided that an interval of one year had elapsed. The Prime Minister admitted that the Lords had not been obstructive but declared: "We do not wait today for a disease to break out, but try to cure it in advance." It was generally believed at the time that the bill was designed to secure the passage of a projected bill to nationalize the iron and steel industry during the life of the existing parliament, despite the opposition that might develop in the House of Lords. The Parliament Bill had a relatively quiet passage when compared with the storm caused by its predecessor, and it became law in 1949. It proved unnecessary to use its provisions to carry the Iron and Steel Bill through the House of Lords, for the latter agreed to accept it with the understanding that its operation would be suspended until after the general election.

Electoral Reform Once More.   Another legislative achievement of the Labor party was the passage of the Representation of the People Act of 1948. It was described by the Home Secretary, Chuter Ede, as completing "the progress of the British people towards a full and complete democracy begun by the Great Reform Bill of 1832" because it wiped out "the last of the privileges that have been retained by special classes in the franchise of this country." Its effects on the size of the electorate and the conduct of elections were much less than those of the earlier reform acts. These were the most important changes: (1) the residence period required for registration was eliminated; (2) the business premises franchise and the university franchise were abolished; and (3) there was a complete redistribution of seats. The chief innovation here was the destruction of the last of the two-member constituencies, including the City of London. The number of seats, which had been 640, was reduced to 625, and each constituency had a voting population of about 56,000.

General Elections after the Act of 1948. Apparently the Labor party suffered more than the Conservatives from the redistribution. The effect of the Act of 1948 as a whole, when coupled with a tendency toward greater rigidity of voting habits, seems to have been one of crushing minor parties still further without giving the major parties working majorities. In the general election of 1950 the Labor party secured a majority of only 6 over all other parties, and the Liberal party elected only 9 members. In spite of the protest of the Conservatives, the Attlee Government put into effect the suspended Iron and Steel Act, but other plans for nationalization were set aside. While the margin of control was slim, the Attlee Government demonstrated how strong party discipline had become when it lasted eighteen months without defeat on a major issue. In the general election of October, 1951, the Churchill Conservatives were returned with a majority of 17 seats over all other parties. They denationalized the iron and steel industry, as well as long-distance road haulage, but otherwise left the edifice of nationalized industries intact. Early in April, 1955, Churchill resigned as prime minister and his place was taken by Sir Anthony Eden. In the general election, held in the following month, the Conservatives received a majority of almost 60 over all other parties, a margin of superiority greater than either of Eden's immediate predecessors had enjoyed.

Regency Legislation. In the years from 1937 to 1953, a series of regency acts were passed that, for the first time, made standing provision for the minority of a sovereign, his incapacity, and his absence from the realm.

In the event of temporary illness or absence from the realm, counsellors of state were to be appointed, but for the minority or total incapacity of a sovereign, a regency was provided. Ordinarily the regent would be the next person in line of succession, who was not excluded by the Act of Settlement and was domiciled in Britain. He must have attained the age of eighteen, if he was the heir apparent; otherwise he must be twenty-one. But if a regency should prove necessary on the succession of a child (under the age of eighteen) of Elizabeth II, who had come to the throne in 1952, and her husband the Duke of Edinburgh, then the latter would be regent. This would also be the case if a regency became necessary during the reign of Elizabeth II. Machinery was set up for declaring and ending a regency if the sovereign should be totally incapacitated. As far as the power of the regent was concerned, he might exercise all the royal functions except that of assenting to a bill which would alter the line of succession to the throne or would alter or repeal an act passed in the reign of Queen Anne for the protection of the Presbyterian Church in Scotland. Thus the ancient monarchy of Britain was further modernized, in this case to ensure as nearly as possible that the royal functions would be carried on despite any emergencies that might affect the person of the monarch.

— 5 —

IRELAND UNDER THE UNION AND AFTER, 1801-1949

In December, 1921, Articles of Agreement for a Treaty between Great Britain and Ireland were signed which profoundly altered the constitutional relationship between the two countries that had been established by the Act of Union in 1800. Under these Articles, Ireland, which was styled the Irish Free State, was to have its own parliament and an executive responsible to that parliament and to enjoy the same constitutional status within the British Empire as Canada, Australia, New Zealand, and the Union of South Africa. The Irish Free State was to include all of Ireland, though permission was given to Northern Ireland to remain outside the jurisdiction of the Irish Free State if it so desired. Northern Ireland as a political entity had come into existence under an act of the British parliament passed in 1920. It availed itself of this permission and continued its constitutional relationship with Great Britain as part of the United Kingdom of Great Britain and Northern Ireland. For a time the Irish Free State maintained steadily weakening ties with the United Kingdom, but these ended after the Second World War, when in 1949 the Irish Free State became formally the Irish Republic, totally independent of the British crown.

Anglo-Irish Relations in the Middle Ages. The creation of the Irish Free State was due to the failure of British statesmanship to solve the "Irish Question." This was a complex of problems bound up with the long history of Anglo-Irish relations that began in the late twelfth century when Henry II was accepted as feudal suzerain by various Anglo-Norman barons and adventurers, who had extended their sway over parts of Ireland, and also by some Irish chieftains. Dublin became the Anglo-Norman capital, and Anglo-Norman institutions were introduced into Ireland: a lord lieutenant representing the king, a privy council, a parliament, a chancery, an exchequer, law courts, and, in the thirteenth century, the English common law. The kings of England from John to Henry VIII were styled lords of Ireland until the latter, under an act of the Irish parliament, took the title of King of Ireland.

Poynings' Law. Royal control over the Irish parliament had been strengthened in the previous reign. During the Wars of the Roses in England, Yorkist sentiment had become very strong in Ireland. Fearing that a powerful lord lieutenant might utilize it to seize Ireland, Henry VII sent over a trusted lord lieutenant in the person of Sir Edward Poynings, who summoned an Irish parliament, which passed the famous Poynings' Law in 1495. By this no Irish parliament could be held thereafter except with the prior consent of the king and his privy council in England, and its legislative power was confined to accepting or rejecting such bills as had been framed by the Irish privy council and approved by the English privy council. After the Revolution of 1688, members of the Irish parliament prepared heads of bills for submission through these channels, but this effort to recover some legislative initiative was hampered by the need to secure the consent of a variety of authorities, and the legislative initiative of the Irish parliament remained severely circumscribed until the repeal of Poynings' Law by the Irish parliament in 1782.

Rival Claims of the English and Irish Parliaments. The right of the English parliament to legislate for Ireland was repeatedly challenged during the seventeenth century. Irish patriots argued that England and Ireland were coordinate kingdoms, united only by a personal union such as then existed between England and Scotland, and that, therefore, the English parliament had no more lawful authority over Ireland than over Scotland. The Irish challenge was at length met in 1719 when the British parliament passed a declaratory act, in which it asserted roundly its full power and authority to bind the kingdom and people of Ireland in all cases whatsoever. Until its repeal, over sixty years later, this statute continued to remind Ireland of its legislative subordination.

Religious and Agrarian Grievances. Ireland's grievances were not exclusively constitutional. The Reformation in Ireland followed essentially the same lines as that in England, though in Ireland the great majority of the population remained Catholic and loyal to the papacy. The Church of Ireland was a sort of replica of the Church of England, with the king at its head; and the Irish parliament, from which Catholics were excluded, passed penal laws against Catholics paralleling those in England. These were not repealed until the late eighteenth century. Another religious element was added when the so-called Ulster Plantation under James I brought many Scotch Presbyterians to northern Ireland. Unfortunately, economic changes also took place that often coincided with and deepened the religious cleavage. Besides the Protestants in the Ulster Plantation, the suppression of revolts in Ireland gave rise to absentee Protestant landownership throughout the country. No important agrarian reforms came until the second half of the nineteenth century; and, meanwhile, agrarian grievances, *i.e.,* exorbitant rents, evictions, and others, were fertile soil for disturbances and insurrectionary movements.

Grattan's Parliament, 1783-1800. Smarting under their wrongs, Irish patriots under the leadership of Henry Flood and Henry Grattan awaited an opportunity to throw off the control of the British parliament. By 1779 France and Spain were at war with Great Britain; and when British troops were withdrawn from Ireland, a native Irish Volunteer force was formed to protect the country from possible invasion. Its strength was used to exact concessions. In 1782 the Irish parliament was permitted to repeal Poynings' Law, and the British parliament repealed the Declaratory Act. In the following year, the surrender was made more complete when the latter passed the Renunciation Act, explicitly abandoning the claim of a right to legislate for Ireland. From 1783 to 1800 the Irish parliament, sometimes called Grattan's Parliament, occupied a position coordinate with the British parliament. But the Irish executive, headed by the lord lieutenant, was not responsible to the Irish parliament; and the new-found legislative independence meant little without parliamentary reform.

The Catholic Question. In 1793, as war threatened with Revolutionary France, the Irish parliament passed a Catholic Relief Act that repealed the remaining penal laws and conceded suffrage to Catholics on the same terms as Protestants had it. Catholics, however, were not admitted to office or to parliament; and the issue of Catholic Emancipation, as it was called, remained a center of agitation. William Pitt the Younger, who was prime minister, realized that the grant of suffrage should have been accompanied by Catholic Emancipation, but he became convinced that this final concession could be made safely only if the Irish parliament were abolished and Irish representatives were brought to the parliament at Westminster, where they would be in a minority. When rebellion flared in Ireland in 1798, he decided that further delay was too dangerous and that Union and Catholic Emancipation should go hand in hand, the one making the other safe.

Ireland and the Union.   Later the great majority of the Irish people considered the Act of Union (1800) hateful not only because it destroyed the Irish parliament but also because of the extreme corruption by which it was carried through. On the eve of its passage, the Lord Lieutenant, Lord Cornwallis, expressed his detestation of the work in which he was engaged; and the famous historian W. E. H. Lecky later wrote of the Union that it was an English measure, carried "by gross corruption, in opposition . . . to the great preponderance of the unbribed intellect of Ireland." When opposition was early manifested in the unreformed Irish parliament, the Chief Secretary to the Lord Lieutenant, Lord Castlereagh, acted to secure the needed majorities by skillful manipulation of the patronage. At the time, however, Ireland was by no means united in its opposition, for there were Protestants who were less enamored of legislative independence than fearful of their Catholic neighbors, while, as a whole, the Catholics were probably in favor of the measure. It was accepted by their clergy, who expected Catholic Emancipation to follow; and, indeed, Castlereagh was instructed by the British cabinet to solicit the support of Irish Catholics, though without giving direct assurances.

The Act of Union.   On August 1, 1800, the Act of Union became law and went into effect the following January. It provided that the kingdoms of Great Britain and Ireland should be forever united in one kingdom by the name of the United Kingdom of Great Britain and Ireland, with succession to the throne determined as in the Act of Settlement of 1701. In the enlarged parliament of the United Kingdom, Ireland was to be represented in the House of Commons by one hundred members and in the House of Lords by twenty-eight temporal peers and four bishops. These representative temporal peers were to be elected for life from the Irish peerage by their fellow peers, and the remainder of the Irish peers were eligible for election to the House of Commons by an English or Scottish, though not by an Irish, constituency. A further provision united the established churches of England and Ireland and declared that the continuance and preservation of this United Church, as the established Church of England and Ireland, should be deemed a fundamental part of the Union. The principle of free trade was applied to the economic relations between the two countries. (*See Reading No. 30.*)

Catholic Emancipation. If Catholic Emancipation had followed soon afterward, the Union, which was in many ways an equitable settlement, might have been inaugurated with some popular enthusiasm in Ireland. But George III refused even to consider the proposal, and Catholic Emancipation was postponed for a generation. Pitt resigned, and the recurrence of the King's mental illness led him to promise that he would not renew the subject during the latter's lifetime. After he took office a few years later, he was true to his word. When Catholic Emancipation came, it was due to an extra-parliamentary agitation, led by a Catholic barrister, Daniel O'Connell, that compelled the Tory Government of the Duke of Wellington to yield and George IV to give his reluctant assent. Taking advantage of the suffrage granted to Catholics in 1793, O'Connell perfected a Catholic Association that made its strength felt. In 1828, the year in which Protestant Dissenters were relieved of their last important political disabilities, he was elected from County Clare to the parliament of the United Kingdom, from which Catholics were barred by law. Faced with the prospect of civil war in Ireland if Catholic Emancipation should continue to be denied, Wellington, with the aid of Sir Robert Peel, carried legislation in 1829 that removed the political disabilities of Catholics throughout the United Kingdom. (*See Reading No. 31.*)

Political Sentiment in Ireland. Catholic Emancipation probably attached the upper classes of Ireland and the Catholic Church to the British connection, and there was little separatist or republican sentiment on the whole in nineteenth-century Ireland. Though O'Connell never ceased to urge repeal of the Union and the reestablishment of an Irish parliament at Dublin, he desired Ireland to remain within the framework of the British Empire. He encountered, however, the adamant opposition of English statesmen, who increasingly viewed the Union as sacrosanct and considered that nature itself had decreed that neither of the two islands could progress without the other. Although Irish bitterness increased through the years, it was O'Connell's ideals in the main that guided his famous successors in Irish politics. These included Isaac Butt, who founded the Home Government Association in 1870; Charles Stewart Parnell (*see Reading No. 32*), who led both the Land League that sought agrarian reform and the home rulers in the parliament at Westminster, who wanted an independent Irish parliament; and John Redmond, a follower of Parnell, who was the leader of the Irish Nationalists in the early twentieth century. There was some republican and separatist sentiment. It appeared in the Young Ireland movement and in the Fenian Brotherhood, which drew its strength from the anger engendered among Irishmen in the famine years after 1845.

Irish Grievances Lessened.   It was an unsuccessful revolt of the Fenians in 1867 that led Gladstone to carry through parliament an act that disestablished the Church in Ireland, but he had been aware of Ireland's distress long before. As early as 1850, he had described Ireland as "that cloud in the West, that coming storm, the minister of God's retribution upon cruel and inveterate and but half-atoned injustice." It was Gladstone who made the most thorough-going attempt of any Englishman in the nineteenth century to give Ireland justice and atone for past misrule; and had he been able to carry his program in its essentials, Anglo-Irish relations in the twentieth century might well have taken a different turn. In 1869, early in his first administration, he put through parliament an act disestablishing the Church in Ireland; and perhaps for the Irish no aspect of the act was more pleasing than the fact that it made a breach in the Union, of which the Established Church in Ireland had been an integral part. Gladstone also sponsored land acts in 1870 and 1881 that improved the position of the tenant by giving him security against excessive rents and evictions and the right to compensation for improvements. Later, land purchase acts resulted in a great increase in peasant ownership and removed serious agrarian discontent.

Gladstone and Home Rule.   Gladstone made two attempts to give Ireland Home Rule within the Union, one in 1886 and the other in 1893, and he failed both times. The first Home Rule Bill, which he presented to parliament in his third Ministry, provided for an Irish parliament to meet in Dublin and for the removal of Irish members from the parliament at Westminster. This Irish parliament was to have power to legislate generally in domestic affairs, but important areas were reserved for the British parliament, including legislation affecting the crown, peace and war, foreign and colonial relations, customs and excise, trade and navigation, post office, and coinage and legal tender. This Home Rule Bill, which split the Liberal party, was defeated in the House of Commons.

Home Rule seemed dead until public opinion in England swung momentarily in favor of Parnell, the Irish leader, when he was proved to be the innocent victim of some forged letters which *The Times* printed. This current was quickly reversed, however, when he was named a corespondent in a divorce suit in 1890. In Victorian England this meant political disgrace, and Gladstone's refusal to work with Parnell created a division in the Irish parliamentary party that lasted until 1900, when John Redmond succeeded in reuniting it. Meanwhile, Gladstone in his fourth Ministry (1892-1894) tried once more, and again unsuccessfully, to carry through a Home Rule Bill for Ireland. This second Bill differed from the first primarily in retaining Irish members in the parliament of the United Kingdom, although as originally provided they were not to vote on British questions. Gladstone subsequently accepted an amendment to his Bill to permit them to speak and vote on all subjects. This second Home Rule Bill fared better than its predecessor. It passed the House of Commons but was defeated in the House of Lords in September, 1893, after four days of debate. When his Liberal colleagues proved unwilling to face a conflict with the Lords, Gladstone abandoned Home Rule.

Increase in Irish Nationalism. After the fall of Parnell, Irish nationalism became stronger, and there appeared a number of nationalist groups, whose activities were inconsistent with the ideal of Home Rule within the Union. In 1893 a Gaelic League, with Douglas Hyde as president, was formed to foster the revival of the native Irish or Gaelic language, literature, and crafts.

(*See Reading No. 33.*) Its nationalist message was translated into political terms by an association known as Sinn Fein, meaning *Ourselves,* which Arthur Griffith founded in the early twentieth century. It called for non-cooperation with the government and the withdrawal of Irish members from Westminster to form a parliament in Ireland; but it was relatively unimportant until the last years of the First World War.

The Third Home Rule Bill. In 1912 the Liberal Asquith Government introduced a third Home Rule Bill for Ireland. In the preceding year, as will be recalled, the Parliament Act had limited to two years the power of the Lords to delay legislation which the House of Commons was determined upon; and it appeared that the most important stumbling block to Home Rule had been removed. Yet the delaying power of the Lords proved to have serious consequences for Anglo-Irish relations. The Home Rule Bill of 1912 followed the general pattern of the earlier bills. Its gravest defect was its failure to allow for the situation in Ulster, the historic province of northern Ireland where Protestantism was predominant and a much greater industrialization had occurred than in the more agrarian and predominantly Catholic south. The majority of its inhabitants were Unionists who were unwilling to join southern Ireland under the rule of a predominantly Catholic parliament at Dublin, even though its powers were limited. Under the leadership of Sir Edward Carson, the Ulster Unionists organized and armed, pledging in the Ulster Covenant to resist to the death. They were undoubtedly encouraged in their resistance by the Conservative leadership at Westminster. Bonar Law declared, in what was later called the Blenheim Pledge, that he could imagine no length of resistance to which Ulster would go that he and the overwhelming majority of the British people would not support. By the spring of 1914, as the Bill neared its final passage, disaffection was so great among army officers stationed in Ulster that if the Asquith Government had tried to use force to impose Home Rule on Ulster, the weapon might have broken in their hands. In the following September, after Britain had entered the First World War, the Home Rule Bill became law under the Parliament Act; but its operation was suspended by an accomanying statute, and it never went into effect. A truce etween Carson's Ulster Unionists and Redmond's Irish Nationalists permitted Ireland to enter the war with some unity.

Easter Rebellion of 1916. While Ireland as a whole accepted the policy of cooperation, there were some Irishmen who saw Britain's distress as Ireland's opportunity. Among them were members of the Sinn Fein and the Irish Republican Brotherhood, a militant organization whose roots reached back to the Fenians. It was the Irish Republican Brotherhood that organized the Easter Rebellion of 1916, and it was Sinn Fein that profited. Dublin was taken by the insurgents, and a republic was proclaimed, but the Rebellion was a failure. It was unpopular in Ireland until the British government made the mistake of executing the ringleaders, and then Irish public opinion turned against the government. In the following year, Sinn Fein announced its objective as "securing the international recognition of Ireland as an independent Irish Republic"; and in the general election of December, 1918, its candidates, who were pledged to form an Irish national parliament, won a decisive victory over the Irish Nationalists—the party of Parnell and Redmond—who were almost wiped out.

Irish Independence. In January, 1919, a minority of the successful Sinn Fein candidates assembled in Dublin to carry out their program. (The majority were in jail, including Griffith and Eamon de Valera, who had recently emerged as an important leader in the movement.) The proceedings were in Irish. The delegates constituted themselves as the Dail Eireann, *i.e.*, the Assembly of Ireland, proclaimed a national republic, and adopted a constitution. De Valera was chosen president of the new Republic, called Saorstat Eireann or the Irish Free State, meaning thereby an independent Irish Republic. Civil war ensued in Ireland between the republicans and what they regarded as a "usurping" foreign government. It was marked by ugly incidents. The Irish were aroused to intense bitterness and hatred of Great Britain because of the use of the "black and tans," ex-servicemen whose uniforms combined the khaki of the British army with the black caps and belts of the Royal Irish Constabulary.

The Government of Ireland Act, 1920. During the

civil war the Government of Ireland Act of 1920 wa
passed by the British parliament. For the first time Hom
Rule was applied to a partitioned Ireland, and Norther
and Southern Ireland, as its two parts were designated
were given separate parliaments and administration:
Of the two, Southern Ireland, consisting of twenty-si
counties, was much the larger in area and the more pop
ulous, while Northern Ireland included only six of th
nine historic counties of Ulster. The Act of 1920 wen
into effect only in Northern Ireland, which remaine
part of the United Kingdom and continued to be repre
sented at Westminster. Thus Northern Ireland, whicl
had so strenuously resisted Home Rule for a united an
predominantly Catholic Ireland, was the only part of Ire
land in which a Home Rule régime was actually estab
lished. The Act did not go into operation in Souther
Ireland, though an election for which it provided too]
place in 1921; and the victorious candidates, almost ex
clusively members of Sinn Fein, formed the second Dail

Articles of Agreement for a Treaty. In the autumn
of 1921, an Anglo-Irish Conference was held in London
It was attended by delegates chosen by the Irish Repub
lican government and representatives of the British gov
ernment. They agreed to a treaty, which was officiall
styled "Articles of Agreement for a Treaty betwee
Great Britain and Ireland." The conference almost brok
down, and the Irish delegates signed only because o
Lloyd George's threat that failure to do so would lea
to a renewal of the civil war. Under the treaty terms
Ireland was to be known as the Irish Free State, wit]
the constitutional status of a British Dominion. The law
practice, and constitutional usage governing the relation
ship of the British crown and parliament to Canada wer
to be applied to their relationship to the Irish Free State
Northern Ireland was given the opportunity—within
month following the confirmation of the Treaty by th
British parliament—to request that the jurisdiction of th
Irish Free State should not extend to Northern Ireland
This was done, and Northern Ireland remained a part o
the United Kingdom. A further stipulation was that
provisional government should be set up in the Irish Fre
State to act until a new constitution had been adopted
and the Treaty provided the form of an oath that mem

rs of the future parliament of the Irish Free State must ke. They were to swear allegiance to the constitution d were to be "faithful to H.M. King George V, his irs and successors by law." (*See Reading No. 34.*) is requirement later caused much friction between ritain and the Irish Free State, and de Valera in parular was strenuously opposed to it.

The Constitution of the Irish Free State. The eaty was approved by the second Dail in January, 22, by a close vote of 64 to 57, with de Valera leadg the opposition, and given legal effect by the British rliament in the Irish Free State (Agreement) Act of arch 31, 1922. The provisional government was set up d prepared a draft constitution that was approved by third Dail that had been elected to act as a constituent sembly. On October 25 this Constituent Assembly ssed The Constitution of the Irish Free State Act, to nich the Constitution and the Treaty were appended. In is Constituent Act, as it was called, the Constituent Asmbly proclaimed the establishment of the Irish Free ate and declared in effect that the Treaty of 1921 was e supreme law of the land. It provided that if any proision of the Constitution or of any amendment thereof, of any law made thereunder, contravened the Treaty, should be void. In December, 1922, the British Parliaent passed a confirming statute, and in that same month e new Constitution went into effect. It can easily be en that there was opportunity for difference of opinion out the legal origin of the Constitution of the Irish ee State. According to the Irish theory, the Constituent :t of the Irish Constituent Assembly was the legal basis the Constitution, while in the British legal interpretaon it was the British confirming statute that had given legal force.

The most distinctive feature of the Constitution of the sh Free State was the explicitness with which the main atures of responsible government were spelled out. The sponsibility of the cabinet (the executive council) to e dail (the lower house of the legislature) was specid, and provision was made for the appointment of the ime minister (the president of the executive council) the governor general, representing the crown, on the mination of the dail, which virtually meant his elec-

tion by the dail. The Constitution could be eas
amended through legislative action. Under the leadersh
of William T. Cosgrave, who was prime minister of t
Irish Free State during its first decade, the Constituti
was amended to eliminate the crown from the Constit
tion as nearly as possible. Cosgrave's work was co
pleted by his successors.

The Oath. After de Valera became prime minist
in 1932, the Constitution was amended out of all rese
blance to its original character. In particular, he and I
Fianna Fail party, composed primarily of those who h
opposed the Treaty of 1921, were determined to del
from the Constitution the oath that members of the Ir
parliament were required to take. The oath, howev
was required by the Treaty, and so a bill was prepar
that provided both for the removal of the oath fro
the Constitution and the deletion of the article in t
Constituent Act that had elevated the Treaty to the po
tion of the supreme law of the land. When this legis
tion was passed in 1933, it destroyed the very foundati
on which the Irish Free State had been erected. But t
Statute of Westminster, passed by the British parliame
in 1931, had given to the legislature of a Dominion t
right to alter or repeal British statutes applying to t
Dominion, and if the Irish Constituent Act owed
validity to the confirming statute of the British Parl
ment—which in British legal theory it did—then it co
be held that the legislature of the Irish Free State, whi
had the status of a Dominion, was competent to alter t
Constituent Act. This was the view taken by the Judic
Committee of the Privy Council in 1935, in the case
Moore v. the Attorney General of the Irish Free Sta

Other Constitutional Changes. After 1932, un
the direction of de Valera, the Constitution of the Ir
Free State was transformed by amendments. After t
oath had been deleted, appeals to the British privy co
cil were done away with; and in 1936, at the time of t
abdication crisis, the office of governor general, by whi
the crown was represented in the government of the Ir
Free State, was abolished. At about the same time, ho
ever, an External Relations Act was passed that retain
the use of the crown in the appointment of diploma
representatives, the reception of foreign diplomats, a

the conclusion of international agreements, though a circumlocution was used to avoid explicit mention of the king. In 1937 a new Constitution, spoken of as the de Valera Constitution, was adopted, which provided for a republican form of government combined with responsible government. The Irish Free State, hereafter to be called Eire or Ireland, was declared a sovereign, independent, democratic state, but the word "republic" was not used. There was no mention of the king, but the Constitution left undisturbed the External Relations Act of 1936. The British Government promptly declared that it did not regard the new Constitution as altering the status of the Irish Free State, and the Government of Eire made no comment. Subsequently, in 1945, de Valera explained the Irish position. "No lawyer," he said, "would attempt to argue that because of the [Irish] External Relations Act . . . Eire was a Monarchy. . . . We are an independent Republic, associated as a matter of our external policy with the States of the British Commonwealth. To mark this association, we avail ourselves of the procedure of the External Relations Act. . . ."

Formation of the Republic of Ireland. After the Second World War, in which Eire was a neutral, John Costello, its prime minister, announced, in September, 1948, that his government would introduce a Republic of Ireland Bill, which would repeal the External Relations Act of 1936. This meant that Eire was seceding from the British Commonwealth of Nations and breaking the last frail tie with Britain. On December 21, 1948, the Republic of Ireland Act became law in Eire; and on Easter Sunday, April 18, 1949, on the thirty-third anniversary of the Rebellion of 1916, the Republic of Ireland was proclaimed. De Valera refused to join in the celebrations because the republic meant to him, he said, an all-Ireland republic, and there could be no rejoicing so long as Northern Ireland was outside. As for Northern Ireland, its government requested an assurance from Britain that its status in the British Commonwealth would not be changed without its consent.

The Ireland Act of 1949. This assurance was contained in the Ireland Act, which was passed by the British parliament and became law on June 2, 1949. Recognizing that Eire, hereafter called the Republic of Ireland, had ceased after April 18, 1949, to be part of "His Majesty's Dominions," the Act declared that Northern Ireland remained a part of these Dominions and of the United Kingdom and would not cease to be a part without the consent of the parliament of Northern Ireland. Although the last constitutional link between Britain and the major portion of Ireland was broken, the Republic of Ireland, the Act specified, was not to be considered a foreign country, nor were its citizens to be considered as foreigners in the United Kingdom. (*See Reading No. 35.*) Other members of the British Commonwealth also took the stand that the Republic of Ireland was not a foreign country. Thus, the Republic of Ireland assumed with respect to the Commonwealth "an intermediate status between membership and foreignness"; and one more demonstration was provided of the British capacity for compromise in constitutional matters.

— 6 —

THE BRITISH CONSTITUTION IN WORLD HISTORY

In bringing to a close this brief survey of British constitutional history during the last hundred and twenty-five years, we may appropriately ask a simple question that has perhaps occurred to some of our readers and suggest an answer. Most constitutions are of little or no concern except to people who live under them. Why, then, should anybody who lives outside Britain take any interest in the British constitution or its history?

The answer would seem to be implicit in the historical fact that constitutional ideas and practices which originated in Britain have spread throughout the world and become part of the world's political heritage. This has been a result of three main causes—British colonization, British conquest, and British example. (1) Wherever British people have gone as colonists, and they have been the greatest colonizers in history, they have carried with them the general principles of British government. In the words of Gladstone: "There is no parallel in all the records of the world to the case of that prolific British mother, who has sent forth her innumerable children over all the earth to be the founders of half-a-dozen empires. . . . among these children, there is one whose place in the world's eye and in history is superlative: it is the American Republic." (2) British constitutional ideas and practices have been spread among non-British peoples as a result of British conquests. India is the outstanding example here, and it is noteworthy that the present Constitution of India contains a great many provisions derived from the British constitutional system. (3) There has been, from first to last, an immense amount of borrowing from the British constitution in foreign countries. Liberals on the continent of Europe, since before the French Revolution, have looked to Britain as the home of liberty and have associated liberty with the British form of government. It was natural that in setting up new and more liberal governments to take the place of older and more despotic régimes there should have been much borrowing from the British constitution.

Part II

READINGS

— Reading No. 1 —

CHARLES I ON MIXED GOVERNMENT IN ENGLAND, 1642[1]

Charles I's answer to the parliamentary demands embodied in the Nineteen Propositions presented to him by the Long Parliament in 1642, on the eve of the Civil War, was given wide publicity at the time and was often reprinted and referred to later. Though it contains the most authoritative and influential of the early statements of mixed government as the essential characteristic of the English constitution, it has been surprisingly slighted by modern writers on English constitutional history.

There being three kinds of Government among Men, Absolute Monarchy, Aristocracy, and Democracy: and all these having their particular Conveniences and Inconveniences. The Experience and Wisdom of your Ancestors, hath so moulded this out of a Mixture of these, as to give to this Kingdom (as far as humane Prudence can provide) the Conveniences of all three, without the Inconveniences of any one, as long as the Balance hangs even between the three Estates, and they run jointly on in their proper Chanel (begetting Verdure and Fertility in the Meadows on both sides), and the overflowing of either on either side, raise no Deluge or Inundation. The Ill of Absolute Monarchy is Tyranny; the Ill of Aristocracy, is Faction and Division; the Ills of Democracy, are Tumults, Violence, and Licentiousness. The Good of Monarchy, is the uniting a Nation under one Head, to resist Invasion from Abroad, and

[1] *Historical Collections,* ed. by John Rushworth (London, 1692), IV, 731-732.

Insurrection at Home; the Good of Aristocracy, is the conjunction of Council in the ablest Persons of a State for the publick Benefit; the Good of Democracy, is Liberty, and the Courage and Industry which Liberty begets.

In this Kingdom the Laws are jointly made by a King, by a House of Peers, and by a House of Commons chosen by the People, all having free Votes and particular Priviledges. The Government according to these Laws, is trusted to the King; Power of Treaties of War and Peace, of making Peers, of chusing Officers and Counsellors for State, Judges for Law, Commanders for Forts and Castles; giving Commissions for raising Men; to make War Abroad, or to prevent or provide against Invasions or Insurrections at Home; Benefit of Confiscations, Power of Pardoning, and some more of the like kind are placed in the King. And this kind of regulated Monarchy, having this Power to preserve that Authority, without which it would be disabled to preserve the Laws in their Force, and the Subjects in their Liberties and Properties, is intended to draw to him such a Respect and Relation from the great Ones, as may hinder the Ills of Division and Faction; and such a Fear and Reverence from the People, as may hinder Tumults, Violence, and Licentiousness.

Again, That the Prince may not make use of this high and perpetual Power to the hurt of those for whose Good he hath it; and make use of the Name of *Publick Necessity*, for the Gain of his private Favorites and Followers, to the detriment of his People, the House of Commons, (an excellent Conserver of Liberty, but never intended for any share in Government, or the chusing of them that should Govern) is solely intrusted with the first Propositions concerning the Levies of Monies, (which is the Sinews as well of Peace as of War); and the impeaching of those, who for their own Ends, though countenanced by any surreptitiously gotten Command of the King, have violated that Law, which he is bound (when he knows it) to protect; and to the prosecution [*protection?*] of which they were bound to advise him, at least not to serve him in the contrary. And the Lords being trusted with a Judicatory Power, are an excellent Skreen and Bank between the Prince and People, to assist each

against any Incroachments of the other; and by just
Judgments to preserve that Law, which ought to be the
Rule of every one of the Three. . . .

Since therefore the Power, legally placed in both
Houses, is more than sufficient to prevent and restrain
the Power of Tyranny, and without this Power, which is
now asked from Us, We shall not be able to discharge
that Trust, which is the end of Monarchy, since this
would be a total Subversion of the Fundamental Laws,
and that excellent Constitution of this Kingdom, which
hath made this Nation so many Years, both famous and
happy to a great degree of Envy; since to the Power of
punishing (which is already in your hands according to
Law) if the Power of preferring be added, We shall have
nothing left for Us but to look on, since the incroaching
of one of these Estates upon the Power of the other is
unhappy in the Effects, both to them and all the rest;
since this Power of at most a joynt Government in Us
with Our Counsellors (or rather Our Guardians) will
return Us to the worst kind of Minority, and make Us
despicable both at home and abroad, and beget eternal
Factions and Dissentions (as destructive to publick Happiness as War) both in the Chosen, and in the Houses
that chose them, and the People who chose the Chusers;
since so new a Power will undoubtedly intoxicate Persons
who were not born to it, and beget not only Divisions
among them as Equals, but in them Contempt of Us,
as become an Equal to them, and Insolence and Injustice toward Our People, as now so much their In-
feriors, which will be the more grievous unto them, as
suffering from those who were so lately of a nearer degree
to themselves, and being to have Redress only from those
that placed them, and fearing they may be inclined to
preserve what they have made, both out of Kindness and
Policy, since all great Changes are extreamly inconven-
ient, and almost infallibly beget yet greater Changes,
which beget yet greater Inconveniences.

Since as great an one in the Church must follow this
of the Kingdom; since the second Estate would in all
probability follow the Fate of the first, and by some of
the turbulent Spirits Jealousies would soon be raised
against them, and the like Propositions for Reconcilia-
tion of Differences would be then sent to them, as they

now have joyned to send to Us till (all Power being
vested in the House of Commons, and their number making them incapable of transacting Affairs of State with
the necessary Service [*secrecy?*] and Expedition, those
being retrusted to some close Committee) at last the
common People (who in the mean time must be flattered,
and to whom License must be given in all their wild
Humours, how contrary soever to established Law, or
their own real Good) discover this *Arcanum Imperii,*
That all this was done by them, but not for them, and
grow weary of Journy-work, and set up for themselves,
call Parity and Independence Liberty, devour that Estate
which had devoured the rest; destroy all Rights and
Proprieties [*Properties?*], all Distinctions of Families and
Merit; and by this means this splendid and excellently
distinguished Form of Government end in a dark equal
Chaos of Confusion, and the long Line of Our many
Noble Ancestors in a *Jack Cade,* or a *Wat Tyler.*

For all these Reasons to all these Demands Our Answer is *Nolumus leges Angliae mutari.* . . .

— Reading No. 2 —

SIR WILLIAM BLACKSTONE ON THE BRITISH CONSTITUTION, 1765 [2]

*Blackstone's celebrated description of the British con-
stitution is included in the long Introduction he wrote
to Book I of his* Commentaries on the Laws of England,
which was first published in 1765. The Commentaries

[2] Sir William Blackstone, *Commentaries on the Laws of England,* ed. by William Draper Lewis (Philadelphia, 4
vols., 1897), I, 49-51.

became the standard textbook for legal education both in England and in the United States, and his view of the nature of the constitution, though highly theoretical and far from realistic, had vast influence.

✔   ✔   ✔

The political writers of antiquity will not allow more than three regular forms of government: the first, when the sovereign power is lodged in an aggregate assembly, consisting of all the free members of a community, which is called a democracy; the second, when it is lodged in a council, composed of select members, and then it is styled an aristocracy; the last, when it is intrusted in the hands of a single person, and then it takes the name of a monarchy. All other species of government, they say, are either corruptions of, or reducible to, these three. . . .

In a democracy, where the right of making laws resides in the people at large, public virtue, or goodness of intention, is more likely to be found, than either of the other qualities of government. Popular assemblies are frequently foolish in their contrivance, and weak in their execution; but generally mean to do the thing that is right and just, and have always a degree of patriotism or public spirit. In aristocracies there is more wisdom to be found, than in the other frames of government; being composed, or intended to be composed, of the most experienced citizens: but there is less honesty than in a republic, and less strength than in a monarchy. A monarchy is indeed the most powerful of any; for, by the entire conjunction of the legislative and executive powers, all the sinews of the government are knitted together, and united in the hand of the prince; but then there is imminent danger of his employing that strength to improvident or oppressive purposes.

Thus these three species of government have, all of them, their several perfections and imperfections. Democracies are usually the best calculated to direct the end of a law; aristocracies to invent the means by which that end shall be obtained; and monarchies to carry these means into execution. And the ancients, as was observed, had in general no idea of any other permanent form of government but these three: for though Cicero declares himself of opinion . . . [that the best constituted republic is that which is duly compounded of these three forms, the monarchical, aristocratic, and democratic], yet Tacitus treats this notion of a mixed government, formed out of them all, and partaking of the advantages of each, as a visionary whim, and one that, if effected, could never be lasting or secure.

But, happily for us of this island, the British constitution has long remained, and I trust will long continue, a standing exception to the truth of this observation. For, as with us the executive power of the laws is lodged in a single person, they have all the advantages of strength and dispatch, that are to be found in the most absolute monarchy: and, as the legislature of the kingdom is intrusted to three distinct powers, entirely independent of each other; first, the king; secondly, the lords, spiritual and temporal, which is an aristocratical assemblage of persons selected for their piety, their birth, their wisdom, their valor, or their property; and, thirdly, the House of Commons, freely chosen by the people from among themselves, which makes it a kind of democracy: as this aggregate body, actuated by different springs, and attentive to different interests, composes the British parliament, and has the supreme disposal of everything; there can no inconvenience be attempted by either of the three branches, but will be withstood by one of the other two; each branch being armed with a negative power, sufficient to repel any innovation which it shall think inexpedient or dangerous. . . .

— Reading No. 3 —

THE DUKE OF RICHMOND ON PARLIAMENTARY REFORM, 1783 [3]

Charles, third Duke of Richmond, was an advocate of various liberal measures and policies, including concessions to the American colonies and to Ireland as well as parliamentary reform. His high position in the peerage gave weight to his opinions, and his letter to Colonel Sharman, reprinted below in part, appears to have been regarded almost as Holy Writ by parliamentary reformers.

The subject of a parliamentary reform is that which of all others, in my opinion, most deserves the attention of the public, as I conceive it would include every other advantage which a nation can wish; and I have no hesitation in saying that from every consideration which I have been able to give to this great question, that for many years has occupied my mind, and from every day's experience to the present hour, I am more and more convinced that *the restoring the right of voting universally to every man, not incapacitated by nature for want of reason, or by law for the commission of crimes, together with annual elections,* is the only reform that can be effectual and permanent. I am further convinced that it is the only reform that is practicable. . . .

The apprehensions that our government will become too democratic, have been urged on another ground. It

[3] *A Letter from His Grace, the Duke of Richmond, to Lieutenant Colonel Sharman, Chairman to the Committee of Correspondence . . . in Ireland* (London, 1792), pp. 4, 10-11. The document is signed "Richmond" and dated August 15, 1783.

has been said, that the House of Commons has usurped the whole power of government: that the crown in reality no longer possesses its negative, and must in all things be ruled by the House of Commons: that the House of Lords, in consequence of its exclusion (by the will of the House of Commons and not by law) from interfering in money bills, no longer in fact exercises the functions of a branch of the legislature: that the only means by which the balance of the constitution is now in any degree preserved, is by the *irregular* influence of the Crown and of the Peers in the House of Commons: and that if they are totally excluded from interference there, as it is supposed will be the case if this bill passes, and are not restored to their original share of power, the equilibrium will be destroyed, and the Government become purely democratic.

To remedy this objection, it has been answered by others, that it is but just and reasonable, and that they mean at the same time that the Commons are restored to their rights, that the Crown and the Peers should recover theirs. This answer has been ridiculed in my opinion with more wit, than solidity of argument. It has been represented as admitting that whilst the House of Commons continue corrupt, the King and Lords should submit to its decisions; but that when it should really speak the voice of the people, then it would be right to revive the dormant powers of resisting it.

For my part I agree in opinion with those who are for restoring to all parts of the state their just rights at the same time; to do it generally, not partially, is what I must contend for. At the same time, I admit that I am not for restoring the negative of the crown. My reason is, *that it appears to me preposterous that the will of one man should forever obstruct every regulation which all the rest of the nation may think necessary*. I object to it, as I would to any other prerogative of the crown, or privilege of the Lords or people, that is *NOT FOUNDED ON REASON*.

But I agree, that if the House of Commons was reduced to its natural dependence on the people alone, and the present system of making it the exclusive part of government was continued, we should approach to a pure democracy more than our constitution warrants, or

than I wish to see. I am not for a democratic, any more
than for an aristocratic, or monarchic government, solely;
I am for that admirable mixture of the three, that our
inimitable and comprehensive constitution has established. . . .

— Reading No. 4 —

PAINE ON MIXED GOVERNMENT AND REPUBLICANISM, 1791 [4]

The following excerpts are taken from Paine's The
Rights of Man, Part I, *originally published in March,
1791. This was written in reply to Burke's* Reflections
on the Revolution in France, *which had been published
in the preceding year. Paine's polemic was adopted as a
kind of democratic Magna Carta by the British reform
societies and had a great influence in radical circles.*

Reason and Ignorance, the opposites of each other,
influence the great bulk of mankind. If either of these
can be rendered sufficiently extensive in a country, the
machinery of Government goes easily on. Reason obeys
itself; and Ignorance submits to whatever is dictated to it.

The two modes of the Government which prevail in
the world, are, *first,* Government by election and representation: *Secondly,* Government by hereditary succession. The former is generally known by the name of
republic; the latter by that of monarchy and aristocracy.

Those two distinct and opposite forms, erect themselves on the two distinct and opposite bases of Reason

[4] *The Writings of Thomas Paine,* ed. by Moncure D. Conway
    (New York, 1894), II, 382-385.

and Ignorance.—As the exercise of Government requires talents and abilities, and as talents and abilities cannot have hereditary descent, it is evident that hereditary succession requires a belief from man to which his reason cannot subscribe, and which can only be established upon his ignorance; and the more ignorant any country is, the better it is fitted for this species of Government.

On the contrary, Government, in a well-constituted republic, requires no belief from man beyond what his reason can give. He sees the *rationale* of the whole system, its origin and its operation; and as it is best supported when best understood, the human faculties act with boldness, and acquire, under this form of government, a gigantic manliness.

As, therefore, each of those forms acts on a different base, the one moving freely by the aid of reason, the other by ignorance; we have next to consider, what it is that gives motion to that species of Government which is called mixed Government, or, as it is sometimes ludicrously stiled, a Government of *this, that,* and *t'other*.

The moving power in this species of Government, is of necessity, Corruption. However imperfect election and representation may be in mixed Governments, they still give exercise to a greater portion of reason than is convenient to the hereditary Part; and therefore it becomes necessary to buy the reason up. A mixed Government is an imperfect everything, cementing and soldering the discordant parts together by corruption, to act as a whole. Mr. Burke appears highly disgusted that France, since she had resolved on a revolution, did not adopt what he calls *"A British Constitution"*; and the regretful manner in which he expresses himself on this occasion implies a suspicion that the British Constitution needed something to keep its defects in countenance.

In mixed Governments there is no responsibility: the parts cover each other till responsibility is lost; and the corruption which moves the machine, contrives at the same time its own escape. When it is laid down as a maxim, that *a King can do no wrong,* it places him in a state of similar security with that of ideots [*sic*] and persons insane, and responsibility is out of the question with respect to himself. It then descends upon the Minister, who shelters himself under a majority in Parliament, which, by places, pensions, and corruption, he can always command; and that majority justifies itself by the same authority with which it protects the Minister. In this rotatory motion, responsibility is thrown off from the parts, and from the whole.

When there is a Part in a Government which can do no wrong, it implies that it does nothing; and is only the machine of another power, by whose advice and direction it acts. What is supposed to be the King in the mixed Governments, is the Cabinet; and as the Cabinet is always a part of the Parliament, and the members justifying in one character what they advise and act in another, a mixed Government becomes a continual enigma; entailing upon a country by the quantity of corruption necessary to solder the parts, the expence of supporting all the forms of government at once, and finally resolving itself into a Government by Committee; in which the advisers, the actors, the approvers, the justifiers, the persons responsible, and the persons not responsible, are the same persons.

By this pantomimical contrivance, and change of scene and character, the parts help each other out in matters which neither of them singly would assume to act. When money is to be obtained, the mass of variety apparently dissolves, and a profusion of parliamentary praises passes between the parts. Each admires with astonishment, the wisdom, the liberality, the disinterestedness of the other: and all of them breathe a pitying sigh at the burthens of the Nation.

But in a well-constituted republic, nothing of this soldering, praising, and pitying, can take place; the representation being equal throughout the country, and compleat in itself, however it may be arranged into legislative and executive, they have all one and the same natural source. The parts are not foreigners to each other, like democracy, aristocracy, and monarchy. As there are no discordant distinctions, there is nothing to corrupt by compromise, nor confound by contrivance. Public measures appeal of themselves to the understanding of the Nation, and, resting on their own merits, disown any flattering supplications to vanity. The continual whine of lamenting the burden of taxes, however successfully it may be practised in mixed Governments, is inconsistent with the sense and spirit of a republic. If taxes are necessary, they are of course advantageous; but if they require an apology, the apology itself implies an impeachment. Why, then, is man thus imposed upon, or why does he impose upon himself?

When men are spoken of as kings and subjects, or when Government is mentioned under the distinct and combined heads of monarchy, aristocracy, and democracy, what is it that *reasoning* man is to understand by the terms? If there really existed in the world two or more distinct and separate *elements* of human power, we should then see the several origins to which those terms would descriptively apply; but as there is but one species of man, there can be but one element of human power; and that element is man himself. Monarchy, aristocracy, and democracy, are but creatures of imagination; and a thousand such may be contrived as well as three. . . .

— Reading No. 5 —

JEREMY BENTHAM ON THE NEED FOR DEMOCRACY [5]

Bentham became convinced in his later years that the reforms he had at heart would not be carried out under the existing British system of mixed government, and accordingly he became a convert to democracy. The following excerpt is taken from his Constitutional Code, *the principal work of his later years, written between 1818 and 1832. Though this was not published in full*

[5] The Works of Jeremy Bentham, ed. by John Bowring (Edinburgh, 1843), IX, 144-145.

until after his death, its contents were well known to his
followers during his lifetime and much admired by them.

✓   ✓   ✓

In the opinion of a considerable and gradually increasing number of the people, the system of government as
carried on in England, is so bad—so adverse to the
greatest happiness of the greatest number, that a man
desirous of contributing his endeavours to that same
greatest happiness, cannot, without inconsistency, fail of
being desirous of seeing brought about a change:
a change of a nature to add to that greatest happiness,
by substituting good to [*for*] what is evil in the form of
government as it exists at present.

For this purpose two changes are continually brought
to view: one under the name of Parliamentary Reform,
the other under the name of Revolution. By Parliamentary Reform is meant a change in the mode in which
the people are said to be represented: by causing the
men who, under the name of representatives of the
people, exercise a principal share of the powers of government, to be located and dislocable by the great body
whom they are said to represent, instead of a comparatively minute portion of it. By Revolution is meant lo-
cating, in the situation of monarch, an individual different from him by whom it is at present filled.

Parliamentary Reform has been proposed in two
modes:—one styled radical, the other styling itself,
sometimes moderate—sometimes temperate.

By Radical Reform is meant the substituting to [*for*]
the House of Commons, as at present organized, a House
of Commons organized upon the principle of a representative democracy, but leaving in full possession of
their power the Monarch and the House of Lords.

By moderate reform is meant the taking the power
of the House of Commons out of the hands of the present oligarchy, and placing it in a regular and equal sort
of aristocracy, leaving monarch and lords in possession
of their power, as in the former case.

If no good worth contending for—no permanent and
adequate remedy to the existing evils could be brought
about by radical reform, still less could it by moderate
reform.

Note now the change that would be brought about by radical reform: supposing no other change effected than that which is expressed.

The king would remain. Therefore, so long as he retained his power no change would be effected that were [sic] adverse to his interests. But every change that would be beneficial to the interest of the people—contributing to the greatest happiness of the greatest number of them, would, it has been seen, be adverse to his interest. Therefore the king alone would suffice to prevent any considerable good from being done, any effectual remedy from being applied. Take in hand the whole catalogue of abuses. Look over it from beginning to end: not one is there in the continuance of which he has not an interest: not one of them is there which it would not be against his interest to part with: not one of them is there which, on any reasonable ground, he could be expected to part with, if he could help it.

The House of Lords would remain. But of all the members of that house there is not one who, so long as he is one, will not be a sharer in that sinister interest which, as has been seen, stands irremovably attached to the situation of monarch. The House of Lords alone would, therefore, suffice to shut an everlasting door against all remedy.

But if for this purpose the king alone, by his single force, and also the House of Lords alone, by its single force, would either of them suffice, much less can they fail to suffice by their conjunct force. . . .

When on the part of kings and lords, acquiescence has in any way been produced, to leave them in possession of their power, would be to leave them with arms in their hands, in a condition to fight the matter over again. Very generous this indeed, but to whom? To the one and his few hundreds: to these hundreds, generous; but to the many millions, still more ungenerous.

The sources of waste and corruption have all been indicated and enumerated. Dry them up all, dry them up without exception; to [for] all this vast mass of evil you may substitute the opposite and correspondent good, with a sacrifice comparatively inconsiderable of existing interests and expectations. Keep any one of these sources untouched, to produce the same retrenchment, you must make a sacrifice to the same amount elsewhere, at the expense of existing possessions and expectations.

On revolution, considered as a remedy against misrule, a syllable is almost too much. Suppose it effected, what good would be effected by it or with it? Suppose the present king removed, where should we find a better?

Revolution proposed in the character of a remedy, supposes the cause of the evil is in the individual. But it does not lie in the individual: it lies in the species: it lies in the nature of all men, not in the one man who is king.

As well might you think of doing away the mischief of the inquisition system, by removing one grand inquisitor and substituting another in his place. . . .

— Reading No. 6 —

EARL GREY ON THE REFORM BILL, 1831 [6]

The following excerpts are taken from a speech by Earl Grey, the Prime Minister, in the House of Lords on the second reading of the Reform Bill, October 3, 1831.

✓　　　✓　　　✓

My Lords, I hope . . . to prove to your Lordships, that, however easy it be to declaim about dangers and revolutions, there is nothing in this measure which is not founded upon the acknowledged principles of the British constitution—nothing that is not perfectly consistent with the ancient practices of that constitution—and nothing which may not be adopted with perfect safety to

[6] *Hansard's Parliamentary Debates,* Third Series, VII, 934-955.

the rights and privileges of all orders of the state, and particularly of that order to which your Lordships belong; although it has been asserted, with as much confidence as ignorance, that the rights and privileges of your Lordships are particularly endangered by the enactments of this measure. Admitting, then, that something must be done, the question is, what that something ought to be? . . . We had to decide whether, by doing as little as possible, such as bringing in something under the name of Reform, which really meant nothing, we should affect to redeem the pledge we had given, or whether we should adopt . . . the principle . . . of doing something vigorous and effectual. If so, . . . I think we have done so; for our principle is, by doing all that can be justly required, and by honestly redeeming our pledge in the same spirit in which that pledge had been made by us, and understood by the people, to give to the nation contentment, and to all future governments the support of the respectability, the wealth, and the intelligence of the country; which is the surest ground of stability, and nothing short of which can enable a government to make a stand, upon the principles of the constitution, against all wild and unreasonable attempts at innovation. . . . I was satisfied that nothing but a bold and decisive measure would give such general satisfaction and content as would set the question at rest. . . .

. . . The system which prevails in the borough Representation of England is not upheld by any of the writers on our Constitution. On the contrary, it is reprobated by all authority, by all reason, by the statutes, and by the common law of the land. The removal of this vicious and corrupt system, so far from tending to endanger the Constitution, in my opinion, will tend materially to improve and strengthen it. . . .

. . . Though I am the last man . . . to propose to retain the influence which enables any Member in this House to interfere in the elections of Members of the House of Commons—an interference that cannot be too strongly condemned,—yet do I propose that your Lordships should be deprived of any part of your legitimate power or influence? God forbid! The respect due to your rank, and the influence which, from property, you necessarily possess, will belong to you after the passing of the Bill, as fully and in as great a degree as they now do. . . .

— Reading No. 7 —

SIR ROBERT PEEL ON THE REFORM BILL, 1832 [7]

The following excerpt is taken from a speech by Sir Robert Peel, the Tory leader, in the House of Commons on the third reading of the Reform Bill, March 22, 1832.

✓   ✓   ✓

He had stated his reasons for dissenting from the conclusions in favour of this measure of Reform urged by its supporters. He denied that there was any such degree of practical evil attributable to defects in the present constitution of the House of Commons as to justify the hazardous experiment they were about to make, and if there was a necessity for yielding, against their judgment, to a popular demand for Reform, he asserted, that that necessity had been created by the King's Government—by the use which they had made of the King's name, and by their uniform endeavours to increase, instead of to allay, public excitement. He had been challenged to state the specific dangers which he apprehended from this Bill of Reform, and he would obey that call. In his opinion, the Bill would give an additional influence to the democratic power of the State, as distinguished from the monarchy and the House of Lords, so great as to make that power supreme, and virtually, therefore, to convert the mixed government under which we had lived into a simple democracy. He saw no

[7] *Ibid.*, XI, 756-757.

prospect that the King would hereafter be enabled to
exercise an unpopular prerogative, however necessary
that prerogative might be to the permanent interests of
the country. He thought they were about to sacrifice
the means which they then possessed of resisting the first
impulse of the tide of popular opinion. If that tide set
in with a steady unchanging course, it was sure even
then to prevail: but they had at present barriers against
the first shocks which enabled them to outlive a temporary storm of passion, and to yield, if it should become
necessary to yield, with a cautious and gradual relaxa-
tion of the ties and holdings which secured the established
order of things. But hereafter there would be no *vis
inertiae* in the machine of Government—none of that
power of resistance to the restlessness of a desire of
perpetual change which, at present resulted, not only
from the monarchical principle of government, but from
the feelings, habits, and prejudices which were inter-
woven with ancient prescriptive institutions. The power
of the House of Commons would hereafter be supreme;
the other branches of the Legislature would exist merely
by sufferance, until it was discovered that institutions
which had merely the shadow and semblance of authority
were useless and expensive pageants, and had better be
abolished. . . .

— Reading No. 8 —

THE REFORM ACT, 1832[8]

*As the extracts from the Reform Act reprinted below
suggest, the law relating to the distribution of parliamentary seats and to the franchise was not based upon
any general principles. The country was not divided into
equal electoral districts, nor was the principle of universal*

[8] *Statutes of the United Kingdom of Great Britain and Ireland*, LXXII, 154-162: 2 William IV, c. 45.

manhood suffrage adopted. The names of fifty-six boroughs that were totally disfranchised appeared in Schedule A; those of thirty boroughs partially disfranchised appeared in Schedule B; those of twenty-two places that were created boroughs returning two members each appeared in Schedule C; and those of twenty places that were created boroughs returning one member each appeared in Schedule D.

    ✔   ✔   ✔

Whereas it is expedient to take effectual Measures for correcting divers Abuses that have long prevailed in the Choice of Members to serve in the Commons House of Parliament, to deprive many inconsiderable Places of the Right of returning Members, to grant such Privilege to large, populous, and wealthy Towns, to increase the Number of Knights of the Shire, to extend the Elective Franchise to many of His Majesty's Subjects who have not heretofore enjoyed the same, and to diminish the Expence of Elections; be it therefore enacted . . . That each of the Boroughs enumerated in the Schedule marked (A.) to this Act annexed, (that is to say,) *Old Sarum, Newtown, St. Michael's or Midshall, Gatton . . .* , shall from and after the End of this present Parliament cease to return any Member or Members to serve in Parliament.

II. And be it enacted, That each of the Boroughs enumerated in the Schedule marked (B.) to this Act annexed, (that is to say,) *Petersfield, Ashburton, Eye, Westbury . . .* shall from and after the End of this present Parliament return One Member and no more to serve in Parliament.

III. And be it enacted, That each of the Places named in the Schedule marked (C.) to this Act annexed, (that is to say,) *Manchester, Birmingham, Leeds, Greenwich . . .* , shall for the Purposes of this Act be a Borough, . . . ; and that each of the said Boroughs . . . shall from and after the End of this present Parliament return Two Members to serve in Parliament.

IV. And be it enacted, That each of the Places named in the Schedule marked (D.) to this Act annexed, (that is to say,) *Ashton-under-Lyne, Bury, Chatham, Cheltenham . . .* shall for the Purposes of this Act be a

Borough . . . ; and that each of the said Boroughs
. . . shall from and after the End of this present Parliament return One Member to serve in Parliament. . . .

XIX. And be it enacted, That every Male Person of
full Age, and not subject to any legal Incapacity, who
shall be seised at Law or in Equity of any Lands or
Tenements of Copyhold or any other Tenure whatever
except Freehold, for his own Life, or for the Life of
another, or for any Lives whatsoever, or for any larger
Estate, of the clear yearly Value of not less than Ten
Pounds . . . , shall be entitled to vote in the Election
of a Knight or Knights of the Shire to serve in any
future Parliament for the County . . . , in which such
lands or Tenements shall be respectively situate.

XX. And be it enacted, That every Male Person of
full Age, and not subject to any legal Incapacity, who
shall be entitled, either as Lessee or Assignee, to any
Lands or Tenements . . . for the unexpired Residue,
whatever it may be, of any Term originally created for
a Period of not less than Sixty Years . . . of the clear
yearly Value of not less than Ten Pounds . . . , or for
the unexpired Residue, whatever it may be, of any Term
originally created for a period of not less than Twenty
Years. . . . of the clear yearly Value of not less than
Fifty Pounds . . . , or who shall occupy as Tenant any
Lands or Tenements for which he shall be *bonâ fide*
liable to a yearly Rent of not less than Fifty Pounds,
shall be entitled to vote in the Election of a Knight or
Knights of the Shire to serve in any future Parliament
for the County . . . , in which such Lands or Tenements
shall be respectively situate; . . .

XXVI. And be it enacted, That notwithstanding
anything hereinbefore contained no Person shall be entitled to vote in the Election of a Knight or Knights of
the Shire to serve in any future Parliament unless he
shall have been duly registered. . . .

XXVII. And be it enacted, That in every City or
Borough which shall return a Member or Members to
serve in any future Parliament, every Male Person of
full Age, and not subject to any legal Incapacity, who
shall occupy, . . . as Owner or Tenant, any House,
Warehouse, Counting-house, Shop, or other Building,
. . . of the clear yearly value of not less than Ten

Pounds, shall, if duly registered . . . , be entitled to
vote in the Election of a Member or Members to serve
in any future Parliament for such City or Borough:
Provided always, that no such Person shall be so registered in any Year unless he shall have occupied such
Premises as aforesaid for Twelve Calendar Months . . . ,
nor unless such Person, where such Premises are situate
in any Parish or Township in which there shall be a Rate
for the Relief of the Poor, shall have been rated . . . ,
nor unless such Person shall have paid . . . all the
Poor's Rates and assessed Taxes which shall have become
payable from him in respect of such Premises. . . .

— Reading No. 9 —

THE PEOPLE'S CHARTER, 1837[9]

*William Lovett was the principal author of "The
People's Charter" and one of the most important leaders
of the Chartist movement. In his autobiography,* Life
& Struggles of William Lovett, *he tells how he drafted
the document with the aid of a number of the disciples
of Jeremy Bentham. Its most important portions are
reprinted here.*

✓   ✓   ✓

Be it therefore Enacted,
That from and after the passing of this Act, every
male inhabitant of these realms be entitled to vote for
the election of a Member of Parliament, subject however to the following conditions.—

[9] Reprinted in *The Chartist Circular,* no. 2, Glasgow, October 5, 1839.

1. That he be a native of these realms, or a foreigner who has lived in this country upwards of two years, and been naturalized.

2. That he be twenty-one years of age. . . .

ELECTORAL DISTRICTS

I. Be it enacted, that for the purpose of obtaining an equal representation of the people in the Commons' House of Parliament, the United Kingdom be divided into 300 electoral districts.

II. That each such district contain, as nearly as may be, an equal number of inhabitants. . . .

V. That each electoral district return one representative to sit in the Commons' House of Parliament, and no more. . . .

ARRANGEMENT FOR NOMINATIONS

I. Be it enacted . . . that all nominations be taken as hereinafter directed. . . .

XI. That no other qualification shall be required for members to serve in the Commons' House of Parliament than the choice of the electors.

ARRANGEMENT FOR ELECTIONS

I. Be it enacted, that a general election of Members of Parliament for all the electoral districts of the United Kingdom take place on the first Monday in June in each year; and that all vacancies by death, resignation, or otherwise, shall be filled up as nearly as possible within eighteen days after they occur. . . .

XIII. That when any voter's certificate [*signifying registration*] is examined by the registration clerk and found to be correct, he shall be allowed to pass on to the next barrier, where a balloting ball shall be given to him by the person appointed for that purpose; he shall then pass on to the balloting box, and with all due dispatch shall put the balloting ball into the aperture opposite the name of the candidate he wishes to vote for, after which, he shall, without delay, leave the room by the door assigned for the purpose. . . .

DURATION OF PARLIAMENT

I. Be it enacted, that the Members of the House of Commons chosen as aforesaid, shall meet on the first Monday in June in each year, and continue their sittings from time to time as they may deem it convenient, till the first Monday in June following, when the next new Parliament is to be chosen: they shall be eligible to be re-elected. . . .

PAYMENT OF MEMBERS

I. Be it enacted, that every Member of the House of Commons be entitled, at the close of the session, to a writ of expenses on the Treasury, for his legislative duties in the public service, and shall be paid £ 500 per annum. . . .

— Reading No. 10 —

WALTER BAGEHOT ON CABINET GOVERNMENT[10]

Bagehot's famous book, The English Constitution, *consisting of his magazine articles that had already appeared, was first published in 1867, just before the Reform Bill of that year. It has often been reprinted and has been appropriately included in* The World's Classics *series, with an illuminating introduction by the Earl of Balfour. Bagehot's main object was to describe the British constitutional system as it was actually working when he wrote, to examine existing constitutional realities in contrast to what he called "the literary theory" of the con-*

[10] *The Works of Walter Bagehot,* ed. by Forrest Morgan (Hartford, Conn., 1889), IV, 59-63.

stitution. The part of the British constitution which most interested him, and which had been perhaps most obscured by the literary theory, was the cabinet system.

✦ ✦ ✦

The efficient secret of the English Constitution may be described as the close union, the nearly complete fusion, of the executive and legislative powers. No doubt by the traditional theory, as it exists in all the books, the goodness of our Constitution consists in the entire separation of the legislative and executive authorities; but in truth its merit consists in their singular approximation. The connecting link is *the Cabinet*. By that new word we mean a committee of the legislative body selected to be the executive body. The legislature has many committees, but this is its greatest. It chooses for this, its main committee, the men in whom it has most confidence. It does not, it is true, choose them directly; but it is nearly omnipotent in choosing them indirectly. . . . As a rule, the nominal Prime Minister is chosen by the legislature, and the real Prime Minister for most purposes—the leader of the House of Commons—almost without exception is so. There is nearly always some one man plainly selected by the voice of the predominant party in the predominant House of the legislature to head that party, and consequently to rule the nation. We have in England an elective first magistrate as truly as the Americans have an elective first magistrate. The Queen is only at the head of the dignified part of the Constitution; the Prime Minister is at the head of the efficient part. . . .

The leading minister so selected has to choose his associates, but he only chooses among a charmed circle. The position of most men in Parliament forbids their being invited to the Cabinet; the position of a few men insures their being invited. Between the compulsory list whom he must take, and the impossible list whom he cannot take, a Prime Minister's independent choice in the formation of a Cabinet is not very large; it extends rather to the division of the Cabinet offices than to the choice of Cabinet ministers. Parliament and the nation have pretty well settled who shall have the first places; but they have not discriminated with the same accuracy which man shall have which place. . . .

The Cabinet, in a word, is a board of control chosen by the legislature, out of persons whom it trusts and knows, to rule the nation. The particular mode in which the English ministers are selected; the fiction that they are, in any political sense, the Queen's servants; the rule which limits the choice of the Cabinet to the members of the legislature,—are accidents unessential to its definition, historical incidents separable from its nature. Its characteristic is, that it should be chosen by the legislature out of persons agreeable to and trusted by the legislature. Naturally, these are principally its own members; but they need not be exclusively so. A Cabinet which included persons not members of the legislative assembly might still perform all useful duties. Indeed, the peers, who constitute a large element in modern Cabinets, are members nowadays only of a subordinate assembly. The House of Lords still exercises several useful functions; but the ruling influence, the deciding faculty, has passed to what, using the language of old times, we still call the "lower House,"—to an assembly which, though inferior as a dignified institution, is superior as an efficient institution. . . .

But the detail of the composition of a Cabinet, and the precise method of its choice, are not to the purpose now; the first and cardinal consideration is the definition of a Cabinet. We must not bewilder ourselves with the separable accidents until we know the necessary essence. A Cabinet is a combining committee,—a *hyphen* which joins, a *buckle* which fastens, the legislative part of the state to the executive part of the state. In its origin it belongs to the one, in its functions it belongs to the other.

The most curious point about the Cabinet is, that so very little is known about it. The meetings are not only secret in theory, but secret in reality. By the present practice, no official minute in all ordinary cases is kept of them; even a private note is discouraged and disliked. The House of Commons, even in its most inquisitive and turbulent moments, would scarcely permit a note of a Cabinet meeting to be read; no minister who respected the fundamental usages of political practice would attempt to read such a note. . . .

But a Cabinet, though it is a committee of the legislative assembly, is a committee with a power which no assembly would—unless for historical accidents, and after happy experience—have been persuaded to intrust to any committee. It is a committee which can dissolve the assembly which appointed it; it is a committee with a suspensive veto, a committee with a power of appeal. Though appointed by one Parliament, it can appeal if it chooses to the next. Theoretically, indeed, the power to dissolve Parliament is intrusted to the sovereign only, and there are vestiges of doubt whether in *all* cases a sovereign is bound to dissolve Parliament when the Cabinet asks him to do so; but neglecting such small and dubious exceptions, the Cabinet which was chosen by one House of Commons has an appeal to the next House of Commons. The chief committee of the legislature has the power of dissolving the predominant part of that legislature,—that which at a crisis is the supreme legislature. The English system, therefore, is not an absorption of the executive power by the legislative power: it is a fusion of the two. Either the Cabinet legislates and acts, or else it can dissolve. It is a creature, but it has the power of destroying its creators. It is an executive which can annihilate the legislature, as well as an executive which is the nominee of the legislature. It *was* made, but it *can* unmake; it was derivative in its origin, but it is destructive in its action. . . .

— Reading No. 11 —

EDWARD GIBBON WAKEFIELD ON THE ESSENTIAL CHARACTERISTICS OF THE BRITISH CONSTITUTION, 1844 [11]

In the article by Wakefield from which excerpts are given below he pointed out that the ministry was responsible to the House of Commons alone and that the House of Lords occupied a subordinate position. Wakefield understood that there existed in the British constitutional system what later came to be called a safety-valve, namely, the power of the crown, acting on ministerial advice, to create peers for the purpose of passing a bill in the House of Lords.

The really essential features of the British Constitution, to which everything else in it is altogether secondary, are two in number. The first consists in its mode of reducing to practice, by means of a strictly-defined and jealously-maintained system of ministerial responsibility, the old maxim that "the King can do no wrong," that his acts and intentions must always be right, and may not, under any circumstances, be so much as imagined to be otherwise. The maxim itself is one of very ancient date, . . . it may be said to be the first instinct of that unreflecting loyalty which invites, and, in the history of the world, has so often produced, despotism. So, too, is the notion of ministerial accountability an old one, perpetually acted upon in fact in all countries, wherever, under the pressure of real or fancied injury, people's loyalty or

[11] Edward Gibbon Wakefield, "Sir Charles Metcalfe in Canada," reprinted in E. M. Wrong, *Charles Buller and Responsible Government* (Oxford, 1926), pp. 185-190. Reprinted by permission of Oxford University Press.

cowardice have not been strong enough to keep them true to the faith of non-resistance. . . .

The second grand characteristic of the Constitution, is to be found in the admitted practical ascendancy of the House of Commons. . . . To all practical intents, the House of Commons, though in theory but the third estate of the realm, has become the representative embodiment of the nation as a whole. The Upper House is the special representative of the aristocracy, a grand council of revision less amenable than the Lower House to popular control, with higher rank and more show of privilege, but having far less of the reality of power. The Sovereign, as the supreme head of the nation, secure in the responsibility of his Ministers, retains unquestioned every Prerogative required for the administration of its affairs. If his Ministers cannot so shape their course, as to carry with them the House of Commons, they either must induce him to dissolve the House, or must resign; for the powers of the House are such, that without assailing the Prerogative, or so much as threatening a single Minister with impeachment, it can make the government of the country impossible, in the extreme case of a determined refusal of the Ministry to meet its wishes. It can stop the supplies, and refuse to pass the yearly Mutiny Bill. The Sovereign may still choose and command his servants as before; but, except so far as the Civil List goes, he can no longer pay, and ceasing to pay, can besides no longer punish them. His very army and navy on a given day would stand released from every obligation of discipline. From the extent of this power, it necessarily follows, that its exercise is really never thought of. Long before things come to this pass, a Ministry not having the confidence of the House, always finds itself under the practical necessity of retiring, or trying what it can do with a new House. Should the new House too prove adverse, the struggle is at an end. No Ministers so outvoted would dare cling to office; and the Sovereign has therefore to find others to take their places, and do for him what they have failed to do.—The House of Lords has no such power as this. It may modify the policy of Ministers, or may greatly embarrass them (provided they are not overwhelmingly strong in the support of the House of Commons), by placing its veto on their measures; but it cannot turn them out, so long as the Commons are their friends, or are even willing to let them stay in office. Against the determined will of the Commons, backed by the public voice, it cannot for any length of time make a successful stand, even in its veto of a legislative measure; for, as the Commons virtually control the Ministry, and the Crown can always create Peers, there is ever a quiet influence at work tending to assimilate the Upper to the Lower House. And in any crisis of peculiar urgency, such for instance as occurred in the days of the Reform Bill, it is always within the power of the latter to insist upon the exertion of that influence to any extent that may be necessary to secure the end in view.

Such, I repeat, are the two cardinal principles of the Constitution, the strict adherence to which is absolutely essential to its existence; the first, that Ministers must assume the entire responsibility of every act of the Crown while they remain in office; the second, that the popular branch of the Legislature must have that ascendancy in the State which will enable it to force them out of office, if the acts and principles they appear before it to defend, are such as it is disposed deliberately to condemn. . . .

— Reading No. 12 —

LORD LYNDHURST ON THE LORDS' VETO, 1858 [12]

Lord Lyndhurst, who had been active in the House of Lords in opposing Whig legislative measures in the 1830's after the passing of the Great Reform Bill, explained toward the end of his parliamentary career his conception

[12] *Hansard's Parliamentary Debates,* Third Series, CXLIX, 1770 f.

*of the proper relationship between the Lords and the
Commons. The lingering influence of the ideas of mixed
government is apparent in his speech on Jewish Relief,
delivered on April 27, 1858, from which the following
excerpts are taken.*

      ✔   ✔   ✔

I have told you that Bills for the admission of the Jews
have been passed in the other House with great and increasing majorities; but in this House those Measures
have been from time to time rejected by very small and
inconsiderable majorities; in no instance being more than
one-tenth of the number of persons who were called on
to vote on the subject. . . .

Our Legislature is a species of progressive machine; it
consists of three independent powers; and, if each power
adhere rigidly to its own opinion, the machinery of legislation would on many occasions come to a standstill; it
is by mutual forbearance and concession that the machine practically works out the great objects of the constitution. I desire to impress this consideration most
strongly upon your Lordships, and I have on more than
one occasion expressed my opinion with respect to the
particular position and duty of the House of Lords. It is
part of our duty to originate legislation, but it is also a
most important part of our duty to check the inconsid-
erate, rash, hasty, and undigested legislation of the other
House; to give time for consideration; and for consulting,
and perhaps modifying the opinions of the constituencies; but I never understood, nor could such a principle
be acted upon, that we were to make a firm, determined,
and persevering stand against the opinion of the other
House of Parliament, when that opinion is backed by the
opinion of the people, and least of all, on questions affecting, in a certain degree, the constitution of that House
and popular rights. If we do make such a stand, we ought
to take care that we stand on a rock. . . .

— Reading No. 13 —

GLADSTONE ON REFORM OF THE BOROUGH FRANCHISE, 1864[13]

The following excerpts are taken from a speech by Gladstone in the House of Commons on May 11, 1864, in support of a motion for the second reading of a bill to extend the borough franchise. This speech, which excited considerable comment at the time, associated Gladstone prominently with parliamentary reform.

✔   ✔   ✔

We are told that the working classes do not agitate for an extension of the franchise; but is it desirable that we should wait until they do agitate? In my opinion, agitation by the working classes, upon any political subject whatever, is a thing not to be waited for, not to be made a condition previous to any Parliamentary movement; but, on the contrary, it is a thing to be deprecated, and, if possible, anticipated and prevented by wise and provident measures. . . .

. . . The objection made by the hon. Gentleman opposite and by many others is, that the working classes, if admitted even in limited numbers, or at all events so as to form any considerable proportion of a constituency, will go together as a class, and wholly separate themselves from other classes. I do not wish to use harsh language, and therefore I will not say that that is a libel; but I believe it to be a statement altogether unjustified by reference to facts. It is not a fact, as I believe, that the working men who are now invested with the franchise, act together as a class; and there is not the slightest reason to suppose that they would so act together if there were a moderate and fair extension of the suffrage. . . . I appeal to the evidence of all, who know anything of the facts, to say whether we have not

[13] *Ibid.,* CLXXV, 317 ff.

seen the working classes, in places where they possessed
the franchise, instead of being disposed to go together
as a class, rather inclined, as a general rule, and under
all ordinary circumstances, to follow their superiors, to
confide in them, to trust them, and to hold them in high
esteem. Their landlords in the country, their employers
in the town, their neighbours and those whose personal
characters they respect—these are the men whom the
working classes commonly elect to follow; and for my
part, I believe, if there is anything which will induce
them to alter their conduct, and to make it their rule to
band together as a class, it will be resentment at exclusion, and a sense of injustice. . . .

. . . Is it right, I ask, that, in the face of such disposi-
tions, the present law of almost entire exclusion should
continue to prevail? . . . I venture to say that every
man who is not presumably incapacitated by some consideration of personal unfitness or of political danger is
morally entitled to come within the pale of the Constitution. . . .

The present franchise, I may add, on the whole—subject, of course, to some exceptions—draws the line between the lower middle class and the upper order of the
working class. As a general rule, the lower stratum of
the middle class is admitted to the exercise of the franchise, while the upper stratum of the working class is
excluded. That I believe to be a fair general description
of the present formation of the constituencies in boroughs and towns. Is it a state of things, I would ask,
recommended by clear principles of reason? Is the upper
portion of the working classes inferior to the lowest portion of the middle? . . . For my own part, it appears to me
that the negative of the proposition may be held with the
greatest confidence. . . .

And now, Sir, one word in conclusion. I believe that
it has been given to us of this generation to witness, ad-
vancing as it were under our very eyes from day to day,
the most blessed of all social processes; I mean the process which unites together not the interests only but the
feelings of all the several classes of the community, and
which throws back into the shadows of oblivion those
discords by which they were kept apart from one another. I know of nothing which can contribute, in any

degree comparable to that union, to the welfare of the
commonwealth. It is well, Sir, that we should be suitably
provided with armies, and fleets, and fortifications; it is
well too that all these should rest upon and be sustained,
as they ought to be, by a sound system of finance, and
out of a revenue not wasted by a careless Parliament, or
by a profligate Administration. But that which is better
and more weighty still is that hearts should be bound together by a reasonable extension, at fitting times, and
among selected portions of the people, of every benefit
and every privilege that can justly be conferred upon
them. . . .

— Reading No. 14 —

DISRAELI AND PARLIAMENTARY REFORM, 1867 [14]

*In his speech of March 18, 1867, Disraeli explicitly
denied that the object of the Reform Bill was to introduce democracy. Excerpts from his speech given below
show that he planned to extend the franchise primarily
in the boroughs and to only a portion of the working
classes there. This concession, moreover, was to be balanced by extra votes for the middle classes. These "fancy
franchises" disappeared in the face of Liberal criticism
in the House of Commons, and the final measure democ-
ratized the borough franchise.*

✓   ✓   ✓

Sir, I rise to ask leave to introduce a Bill further to
amend the Laws for regulating the Representation of the
People in Parliament. . . . I propose . . . to confine

[14] *Ibid.*, CLXXXVI, 6-25.

my observations to two points. I will endeavour, in the
first place, clearly to convey to the House the object of
the Government in the Bill which I am asking leave to
introduce; and secondly, I will detail the means by which
that purpose, in their opinion, can be accomplished. It
will be for the House, first, to decide whether that object
is desirable; and secondly, if desirable, whether the means
which we propose are adequate; and, in the first place, I
would say that our object is not only to maintain, but to
strengthen, the character and functions of this House.
They are peculiar in any popular assembly; not only rare,
but perhaps unexampled in any other which has existed.
The House of Commons has combined national representation with the attributes of a Senate. That peculiar union has, in our opinion, been owing to the variety of
elements of which it is formed. Its variety of character
has given to it its deliberative power, and it owes to its
deliberative power its general authority. We wish, I repeat, not only to maintain, but to strengthen that character and those functions; and we believe that, in the present age and under the existing circumstances of the
country, the best way to do so is to establish them on a
broad popular basis. I know that there are some persons
in whose minds the epithet which I have just used may
create a feeling of distrust; but I attribute the sentiment
of alarm which is associated with it to a misapprehension
of its meaning, and to that perplexity of ideas which too
often confounds popular privileges with democratic
rights. They are not identical: they are not similar. More
than that, they are contrary. Popular privileges are consistent with a state of society in which there is great in-
equality of condition. Democratic rights, on the contrary,
demand that there should be equality of condition as the
fundamental basis of the society which they regulate.
Now, that is, I think, a distinction which ought to be
borne in mind by the House in dealing with the provisions of the Bill which I am about to ask leave to introduce. If this Bill be a proposal that her Majesty shall be
enabled to concede to her subjects, with the advice and
concurrence of her Parliament, a liberal measure of popular privileges, then there may be many of its provisions
which will be regarded as prudent, wise and essentially
constitutional. If, on the other hand, it be looked upon

as a measure having for its object to confer democratic rights, then I admit much that it may contain may be viewed in the light of being indefensible and unjust. We do not, however, live,—and I trust it will never be the fate of this country to live—under a democracy. The propositions which I am going to make to-night certainly have no tendency in that direction. Generally speaking, I would say that, looking to what has occurred since the Reform Act of 1832 was passed—to the increase of population, the progress of industry, the spread of knowledge, and our ingenuity in the arts—we are of opinion that numbers, thoughts, and feelings have since that time been created which it is desirable should be admitted within the circle of the Constitution. We wish that admission to take place in the spirit of our existing institutions, and with a due deference to the traditions of an ancient State.

In dealing with the question of the distribution of power in such a State . . . , I would, in the first place, call the attention of the House to that part of it which is perhaps the most important, and which certainly, to the greatest extent commands the interest of the public. I allude to the franchise, and especially that which should prevail in towns. I would ask the House at the outset to consider the principles upon which the occupation franchise in boroughs ought to rest, and upon which it is expedient to base it. In 1832 the borough franchise was founded on the principle of value. Those who paid £10 for the house in which they lived, subject to certain regulations as regards rates and residence, had the borough franchise conferred upon them. . . . We believe that the House has resolved and wishes that the borough suffrage should be bound up and united with the duty of paying rates for the maintenance of the poor . . . . beneath the £10 line which now qualifies there are 237,000 persons who are rated to the poor and who pay rates, and who if the law were so changed that value should not be an element would then be qualified to vote for Members of Parliament. Now, if you add these 237,000 persons who are rated to the poor, and who pay their rates, to the 644,000 who are at present qualified, you will find that there would be 881,000 persons, fulfilling the required conditions—that is to say, almost exactly two-thirds of the whole of the householders in the boroughs of England and Wales. There would still remain 486,000, who would not be qualified under these circumstances, because they do not pay rates personally. . . .

. . . But it is said, and it has been said by a very high authority . . . that the plan of the Government . . . was an assault upon the rights and power of the middle classes. It is certainly not the intention of Her Majesty's Government to introduce a measure which shall make such an assault. Her Majesty's Government are anxious that, on the one hand, the aristocracy, and on the other hand the working classes, shall have their due share in the Parliamentary constitution of the country; but they recognize with sincerity the extreme expediency of the principle that the influence of the middle classes of the country should not be diminished. The Government look to the steady virtues of those classes to exercise a right bias on the constitution of the country. . . . But if there be . . . any chance such as has been intimated by this great authority, why, I think that we meet it by a proposition to institute a franchise . . . founded on the payment of direct taxation. We propose that every person in England who pays 20 s. a year direct taxation shall possess a vote. . . . if he is also a householder, and pays his rates, [he] may exercise his suffrage in respect of both qualifications. . . .

There are other franchises which we also propose. . . . The vote which we wish to found upon the possession of £50 property in the funds or of £50 in savings-banks constitutes property qualifications of this character; that is to say, we will give to small holders of personal property the same privileges which the small holders of real property have. . . .

. . . I am told that in this measure there are checks and counterpoises, and that it assumes in this country the existence of classes. If there are checks and counterpoises in our scheme, we live under a Constitution of which we boast that it is a Constitution of checks and counterpoises. If the measure bears some reference to existing classes in this country, why should we conceal from ourselves . . . the fact that this country is a country of classes, and a country of classes it will ever remain?

— Reading No. 15 —

SIDNEY LOW ON THE HOUSE OF COMMONS[15]

Sidney Low was an author, journalist, and minor historian, who is best remembered today for his master-piece, The Governance of England, *which was published in 1904. The essence of the English system of government, he concluded, was that it was in a state of constant development. Thus the picture drawn by Bagehot for the middle period of the reign of Queen Victoria could not be expected to hold true for the early years of the twentieth century. One of the most remarkable changes noted by Low was the altered position of the House of Commons, which he described in the excerpts printed below.*

✓   ✓   ✓

The House of Commons is the most remarkable public meeting in the world. Its venerable antiquity, its inspiring history, its splendid traditions, its still youthful spirit and energy, the unrivalled influence it has exercised as the model of Parliaments, its inseparable connection with the vitality of the English nation, its place as the visible centre, the working motor of our constitution— all this gives it a unique position. . . .

The law-making function is, if not the oldest, at any rate the most dignified and conspicuous attribute of Parliament, and the one that strikes the popular imagination with the liveliest force. It has so far dwarfed the other powers and duties of the great national Councils that we commonly talk of the two Houses, and sometimes of the Lower House alone, as the Legislature. But when we say that the House of Commons makes the law, we use language that no more conveys the facts than the legal for-

[15] Sidney Low, *The Governance of England* (London, 1919), pp. 55-101. Reprinted by permission.

mula, which tells us that every statute is enacted by the King with the advice and assent of Parliament. New laws are made by the Ministry, with the acquiescence of the majority, and the vehement dissent of the minority, in the House of Commons. The Crown has nothing to do with the matter, the House of Lords very little, except that it has a limited power—seldom exercised in cases of real importance—to delay the operation of the proposed measure; the Opposition party protest against it, energetically but powerlessly at every stage; and the non-official ministerialists are able to do no more than affect the treatment of details.

Every member of the House, with the exception of a score or so who sit on the front benches to the right of the Speaker's chair, would admit, if he spoke the truth, that his influence over legislation was little greater than that of a private individual outside. . . .

The power to shape legislation is in practice confined to those members of the House who form the inner ring of the Cabinet for the time being. . . .

. . . It is of the essence of our existing Parliamentary system, as it has developed in recent years, that votes are not turned. A member of Parliament is elected to vote for a particular Ministry, or to vote against it. He is the delegate of his constituents, or rather of that active section of his constituents which assumes the local management of political affairs. "Your representative," said Burke to the electors of Bristol, "owes you not his industry only, but his judgment, and he betrays, instead of serving, you if he sacrifices it to your opinion. I maintained your interests against your opinions, with a constancy that became me. I knew you chose me to be a pillar of the State, and not a weathercock on the top of the edifice." But that is not at all the view of a representative's functions taken by the members of a modern Liberal or Conservative Association. They do not send him to Parliament to exercise his independence; they would be particularly annoyed and irritated if he did; and they scrutinise his votes with jealous care, in order that they may take him to task speedily, and with no superfluous delicacy or reserve, if he shows any dangerous tendency in that direction.

And the modern M. P. understands the conditions of his political existence so well that, in point of fact, he

hardly ever does vote against his party on any party issue, when his own side is in office. . . .

What has been said of legislation applies largely to
administration. The House of Commons no longer controls the Executive; on the contrary, the Executive controls the House of Commons. The theory is that the
ministers must justify each and all of their acts before
the representatives of the nation at every stage; if they
fail to do so, those representatives will turn them out of
office. But in our modern practice the Cabinet is scarcely
ever turned out of office by Parliament *whatever it does.*
The Ministry may fall by its own connivance as in 1885
and 1895, when it feels that the country is turning against
it; or it may break up on some question, like that of
Home Rule or Free Trade, upon which its own members
are divided. But such a question will be one of policy, not
of administrative action. It is very difficult to bring a
Government to account for anything done in its ministerial work.

The real check upon a too gross and salient misuse of
Ministerial power is, no doubt, the salutary fear of public
opinion. . . . For the control of Parliament, which was
supposed to be regular, steady, and constant, is ex-
changed the control of the electorate, which is powerful
but intermittent. It is brought into operation at uncertain
intervals, and is exercised only with reference to one or
two great issues of policy, often determined by ministers
themselves, instead of being applied, from day to day, to
the conduct of public affairs. . . .

Mr. Bryce tells us that "the House of Commons is
strong because it can call the Ministry to account for
every act, or by refusing supplies, compel their resignation." But the refusal of supplies is a constitutional fig-
ment. "The ultimate legal sanction," says Sir William
Anson, "which the House of Commons could bring to
bear on a Ministry of which it disapproves, the refusal
to pass the Mutiny Act or grant supplies, has never in
fact been applied." . . . Nothing can be better in form
than the separation between the functions of the Committee of Ways and Means and those of the Committee
of Supply, or the manner in which the Estimates are
brought in, presented, and discussed. But in practice the
control of the House is largely inoperative; first because

of the feverish scuffle against time, which forbids deliberate and prolonged examination of detail; and secondly,
because a serious attempt to refuse a Vote, or alter an
item in an account, can usually be foiled by setting the
party machinery to work. . . .

The province of private members in regard to finance
is, in fact, limited to criticism, and there are special reasons why such criticism should be ineffective. The details
are often highly technical. . . .

The selective function is related to the most significant
of all the present activities of the lower chamber of Parliament, that is to say, the business of making and un-
making Ministries. This is now its primary constitutional
office, and no other can be compared with it in real importance. But it does the work indirectly, or it might be
more accurate to say that it lends itself to the work. The
real political sovereign, and the arbiter of the destinies
of cabinets, is the electoral body. In the eighteenth century, Ministries went out of office because they lost the
confidence of the King; in the great Parliamentary period
of the nineteenth century, because they had lost that of
the House of Commons; and under the democratic franchise they have usually taken their dismissal from the
electors. . . .

— Reading No. 16 —

ORIGINS OF THE LABOR PARTY, 1900[16]

*A conference representing the Trades Union Congress
and the leading socialist societies met in Memorial Hall,
London, late in February, 1900. Out of its proceedings
came the Labor Representation Committee, which
adopted the name of Labor party after it elected twenty-*

[16] *The Clarion*, March 3 and 10, 1900.

nine members of Parliament in 1906. The following account of the proceedings is taken from The Clarion, *which G. D. H. Cole, the historian of the Labor party, has called the best and most influential socialist weekly that the British labor movement has as yet produced.*

✓   ✓   ✓

Our readers will remember that the last Trades Congress instructed the Parliamentary Committee to arrange a Conference with other Labour organisations for the purpose of coming to some agreement as to the election of Labour Representatives to the House of Commons.

The Conference took place on Tuesday and Wednesday of this week in the Memorial Hall, London. . . .

Promptly at 12 o'clock the Conference got to work by electing Mr. W. C. Steadman, M. P. for Stepney as chairman. He informed us that there were present 130 delegates, representing 543,316 Trade Unionists, 13,000 I. L. Peers [members of the Independent Labor Party], 9,000 S. D. Fers [members of the Social Democratic Federation], 861 Fabians [members of the Fabian Society].

The Socialist delegates were: S. D. F.: M. Judge, J. Macdonald, H. Quelch, H. R. Taylor. I. L. P.: J. Keir Hardie, Councillor P. Snowden, Ald. F. W. Jowett, J. Burgess, Councillor J. Parker, and J. R. Macdonald. . . .

The Parliamentary Committee [of the Trades Union Congress] had drawn up an agenda embodying suggestions made by the different organisations represented. These suggestions formed the basis of the resolutions discussed by the Conference.

The first one dealt with the object of the Conference, and was in the following words:—

A resolution in favour of working class opinion being represented in the House of Commons by men sympathetic with the aims and demands of the Labour Movement.

To this Mr. Jones, of the Upholsterers, and Mr. Paul Vogel, of the Waiters, wished to add words limiting the Labour representatives to "working men." That is to say, they wish to send no man to Parliament unless he has actually got corns on his hands. The narrow and feeble arguments in support of this policy were swept aside in

one breath by Mr. John Burns, M. P., who protested
that we had had enough of these class distinctions. He
said he was sick of working class boots, and workmen's
trains, and workman's this, that, and the other.

As this seemed to be the view of the meeting the
amendment was not accepted, and the resolution was
eventually passed with the addition of the following
words, proposed by Mr. G. Barnes, of the Engineers:—

> And whose candidatures are promoted by one or
> other of the organised movements represented in the
> constitution which this Conference frames.

The second item on the programme occupied the re-
mainder of the sitting. This dealt with the conduct of the
Labour Group in Parliament. A resolution moved by
Keir Hardie was ultimately adopted. It is as follows:—

> That this Conference is in favour of establishing
> a distinct Labour Group in Parliament, who should
> have their own Whips, and agree upon their policy,
> which must embrace a readiness to co-operate with
> any party which for the time being may be engaged
> in promoting legislation in the direct interest of La-
> bour, and be equally ready to associate themselves
> with any party in opposing measures having an op-
> posite tendency, and further no member of the
> Labour Group shall oppose any candidate whose
> candidature is being promoted in terms of resolution
> No. 1.

The discussion raged round the question as to the principles to be adhered to by the Labour Group, and as to
how much freedom they were to be allowed on matters
outside Labour questions, if any.

The S. D. F., as usual, wished the Group to affirm
their belief in the "class war" and their object as the
Socialisation of all the means of production, etc. (I believe you know the rest) . . . but Joe Burgess and Jim
Sexton for the I. L. P., deprecated the introduction of
abstract principles of an extreme nature into a Conference whose object was to find a working basis for all
parties represented. . . .

So the first day ended, the Conference having resolved

that Labour ought to be represented in Parliament, and
that when it was represented its representatives should
act together as a Labour Group. . . .

The second day of the Conference at the Memorial
Hall last week, was devoted by the delegates to matters
of detail, which included the election of a Joint Commit-
tee. This Committee consists of 12 members—seven
Trade Unionists, two I. L. Peers, two S. D. Fers, and one
Fabian. The following are the names of those elected:
Messrs. Greenall (Miners), R. Bell (A. S. R. S.), P. Cur-
ran (Gas Workers), A. Gee (Textile Workers), A. Wilkie
(Shipbuilding), J. Hodge (Steel Smelters), and F. Rogers
(Vellum Binders), for the Trade Unions; E. R. Pease,
for Fabians; and Keir Hardie and J. Parker, I. L. P. The
S. D. F. delegates had retired when the election was tak-
ing place, and the names of their two committeemen
were not announced.

It was resolved that it should be the duty of the Committee to prepare a list of candidates run in accordance
with Resolution No. 1, to publish this list as the official
candidates of the United Labour Party, and to recom-
mend those candidates for the support of the working-
class electors.

It was also resolved that the Committee should keep
in touch with Trade Unions and other organisations,
local and national, which are running Labour candidates.
That it should call a conference in February of each
year. That it should also report annually to the Trade
Unions Congress and the annual meetings of the national
societies represented on the Committee, and take any
steps deemed advisable to elicit opinion from the members of the organisation to which the Committee is ultimately responsible.

Funds for the new organisation are to be provided by
a payment of 10 s. per 1,000 members of the different
bodies represented. . . .

— Reading No. 17 —

SIR HENRY CAMPBELL-BANNERMAN ON THE HOUSE OF LORDS, 1907 [17]

In his speech of June 24, 1907, supporting his resolution to curb the legislative power of the House of Lords, the Liberal Prime Minister, Sir Henry Campbell-Bannerman, asserted the predominance of the House of Commons and attacked the referendal theory used by the House of Lords in its treatment of Liberal measures.

I rise to move, "That, in order to give effect to the will of the people as expressed by their elected representatives, it is necessary that the power of the other House to alter or reject Bills passed by this House should be so restricted by law as to secure that within the limits of a single Parliament the final decision of the Commons shall prevail." . . .

My Motion affirms the predominance of the House of Commons as the representative House of Parliament, and I submit that in spirit and in fact that is a strictly true constitutional proposition. I may claim for it, up to a point, the adhesion of the Party opposite and of the House of Lords itself. The supremacy of the people is admitted in theory even by the House of Lords. It is admitted that the will of the people . . . is in the long run entitled to prevail. . . . How, then, is that will of the people to be got at and ascertained unless you take the view of the elective House as expressing it? The supremacy of the people in legislation implies in this country at any rate, the authority of the Commons. The party for which I speak has never swerved from that position, and unless you are going to fall back upon some foreign

[17] *The Parliamentary Debates,* Fourth Series, CLXXVI, 909-926.

method, such as the *referendum* or the mandate or the plebiscite, or some other way of getting behind the backs of the elected to the electors themselves, such as was advised by both the first and third Napoleon—unless that is the example you are going to follow, then there is no course open but to recognise ungrudgingly the authority which resides in this House, and to accept the views of the nation as represented in its great interests within these walls. The Resolution embodies, therefore, a principle the logic of which at any rate is accepted by both Parties and both Houses—the principle of the predominance of the House of Commons. . . .

. . . What meaning does the supremacy of the House of Commons convey to the minds of the House of Lords? In the first place, it is matter of common knowledge that its working varies according to circumstances. When their own Party are in power—that is the Party to which the vast majority of the Members of the House of Lords belong—they recognise without reservation, they even make what I would almost call indecent haste, to recognise this supremacy. There is never a suggestion that the checks and balances of the Constitution are to be brought into play; there is never a hint that this House is anything but a clear and faithful mirror of the settled opinions and desires of the country, or that the arm of the executive falls short of being the instrument of the national will. . . .

. . . Witness the transition that takes place the moment a Liberal House of Commons comes into being. A complete change comes over this constitutional doctrine of the supremacy of this Chamber. They rested and reposed on its supremacy during the period I have been dealing with. Now they challenge it; and it becomes a deferred supremacy—a supremacy which is to arrive, it may be, at the next election, or the election after that, or may be never at all. . . . I have never been able to discover, by what process the House of Lords professes to ascertain whether or not our decisions correspond with the sentiments of the electors; but what I do know is that this House has to submit to carry on its existence in a state of suspense, knowing that our measures are liable to be amended, altered, rejected, and delayed in accordance with the mysterious intuition, almost divination, which enables the Lords to keep immediate touch with the electors during a Liberal administration. It is a singular thing, when you come to reflect upon it, that the representative system should only hold good when one Party is in office, and should break down to such an extent as that the non-elective House must be called in to express the mind of the country whenever the country lapses into Liberalism. . . .

Now I come to another question which we have to ask ourselves, and that is: What is the nature of the authority under which the other House, during its intermittent period of activity, claims to override and suspend the decisions of this House and to afford it a merely nominal and deferred predominance? . . . The first thing I would point out is that the merits and demerits of the Bills that we deal with are not in question at all. The Education Bill and the Plural Voting Bill may be thoroughly bad Bills in the estimation of hon. Members opposite. . . . But let hon. Gentlemen observe that the other House, when it proceeded, within twelve months of the election, summarily to dispose of these measures of ours, did so, according to its own account, not on their merits, but because it claimed to know the mind of the country. That was the plea that was urged. "Your Education Bill," they said, "does not square with the professions of the people or the desires of the people, and as for your Electoral Reform Bill, it ought to be part of a larger scheme of reform such as the country desires." . . . We have to take note of this further singular fact that the powers of that House are avowedly exercised without reference to the merits of what is sent up to it, and on the ground that we, who are the representatives of the people as the result of all our elaborate electoral machinery, are incapable of speaking and acting on their behalf. Such a claim will not stand a moment's investigation. The Constitution knows nothing of this doctrine of the special mandate, nothing whatever. It is an invention apparently of the Lords, designed to afford them some kind of shelter behind which they may get rid of the Bills they dislike. . . .

. . . Let the country have the fullest use in all matters of the experience, wisdom, and patriotic industry of the House of Lords in revising and amending and securing

full consideration for legislative measures; but, and these
words sum up our whole policy, the Commons shall prevail.

— Reading No. 18 —

THE CABINET MINUTE ON THE CREATION OF PEERS, 1910[18]

*In the minute reprinted here, the Asquith Cabinet
asked the King for "guarantees" to insure the passage of
the Parliament Bill, if the Liberal party proved successful
in the forthcoming general election. The King had no
recourse but to act on the advice of his ministers, as outlined in this minute, so long as they had a majority in the
House of Commons. This proposed use of the royal prerogative, on ministerial advice, to make possible the passage of a bill through the House of Lords is an interesting
illustration of how ancient royal prerogative powers,
which originally implied no suggestion of democracy,
have been used as modern instruments of democracy.*

✔   ✔   ✔

"The Cabinet has very carefully considered the situation created by the failure of the Conference, in view of
the declaration of policy made on their behalf by the
Prime Minister in the House of Commons on the 14th
of April, 1910.

"The advice which they feel it their duty to tender to
His Majesty is as follows:

"An immediate dissolution of Parliament, as soon as
the necessary parts of the Budget, the provision of Old
Age Pensions to paupers, and one or two other matters
have been disposed of.

[18] Harold Nicolson, *King George the Fifth* (London, 1952),
    p. 136. Reprinted by permission of the publisher.

"The House of Lords to have the opportunity, if they desired it, at the same time (but not so as to postpone the date of the dissolution), to discuss the Government Resolutions.

"His Majesty's Ministers cannot, however, take the responsibility of advising a dissolution, unless they may understand that, in the event of the policy of the Government being approved by an adequate majority in the new House of Commons, His Majesty will be ready to exercise his constitutional powers (which may involve the Prerogative of creating Peers), if needed, to secure that effect should be given to the decision of the country.

"His Majesty's Ministers are fully alive to the importance of keeping the name of the King out of the sphere of party and electoral controversy. They take upon themselves, as is their duty, the entire and exclusive responsibility for the policy which they will place before the electorate.

"His Majesty will doubtless agree that it would be undesirable, in the interests of the State, that any communication of the intentions of the Crown should be made public, unless and until the actual occasion should arise."

— Reading No. 19 —

THE PARLIAMENT ACT, 1911 [19]

In the Parliament Act of 1911, the relationship between the House of Commons and the House of Lords, as this had taken shape in the nineteenth century, was placed on a statutory basis. The most important provisions of the Act are given below.

[19] *Public General Statutes,* XLIX, 38 ff.: 1 & 2 George V, c. 13.

✓   ✓   ✓

Whereas it is expedient that provision should be made for regulating the relations between the two Houses of Parliament:

And whereas it is intended to substitute for the House of Lords as it at present exists a Second Chamber constituted on a popular instead of hereditary basis, but such substitution cannot be immediately brought into operation:

And whereas provision will require hereafter to be made by Parliament in a measure effecting such substitution for limiting and defining the powers of the new Second Chamber, but it is expedient to make such provision as in this Act appears for restricting the existing powers of the House of Lords:

Be it therefore enacted. . . .

1.—(1) If a Money Bill, having been passed by the House of Commons, and sent up to the House of Lords at least one month before the end of the session, is not passed by the House of Lords without amendment within one month after it is so sent up to that House, the Bill shall, unless the House of Commons direct to the contrary, be presented to His Majesty and become an Act of Parliament on the Royal Assent being signified, notwithstanding that the House of Lords have not consented to the Bill.

(2) A Money Bill means a Public Bill which in the opinion of the Speaker of the House of Commons contains only provisions dealing with all or any of the following subjects, namely, the imposition, repeal, remission, alteration, or regulation of taxation; the imposition for the payment of debt or other financial purposes of charges on the Consolidated Fund, or on money provided by Parliament, or the variation or repeal of any such charges; supply; the appropriation, receipt, custody, issue or audit of accounts of public money; the raising or guarantee of any loan or the repayment thereof; or subordinate matters incidental to those subjects or any of them. In this subsection the expressions "taxation," "public money," and "loan" respectively do not include any taxation, money, or loan raised by local authorities or bodies for local purposes.

(3) There shall be endorsed on every Money Bill when it is sent up to the House of Lords and when it is presented to His Majesty for assent the certificate of the Speaker of the House of Commons signed by him that it is a Money Bill. . . .

2.—(1) If any Public Bill (other than a Money Bill or a Bill containing any provision to extend the maximum duration of Parliament beyond five years) is passed by the House of Commons in three successive sessions (whether of the same Parliament or not), and, having been sent up to the House of Lords at least one month before the end of the session, is rejected by the House of Lords in each of those sessions, that Bill shall, on its rejection for the third time by the House of Lords, unless the House of Commons direct to the contrary, be presented to His Majesty and become an Act of Parliament on the Royal Assent being signified thereto, notwithstanding that the House of Lords have not consented to the Bill: Provided that this provision shall not take effect unless two years have elapsed between the date of the second reading in the first of those sessions of the Bill in the House of Commons and the date on which it passes the House of Commons in the third of those sessions.

(2) When a Bill is presented to His Majesty for assent in pursuance of the provisions of this section, there shall be endorsed on the Bill the certificate of the Speaker of the House of Commons signed by him that the provisions of this section have been duly complied with.

(3) A Bill shall be deemed to be rejected by the House of Lords if it is not passed by the House of Lords either without amendment or with such amendments only as may be agreed to by both Houses.

(4) A Bill shall be deemed to be the same Bill as a former Bill sent up to the House of Lords in the preceding session if, when it is sent up to the House of Lords, it is identical with the former Bill or contains only such alterations as are certified by the Speaker of the House of Commons to be necessary owing to the time which has elapsed since the date of the former Bill, or to represent any amendments which have been made by the House of Lords in the former Bill in the preceding session, and any amendments which are certified by the

Speaker to have been made by the House of Lords in the third session and agreed to by the House of Commons shall be inserted in the Bill as presented for Royal Assent in pursuance of this section. . . .

3. Any certificate of the Speaker of the House of Commons given under this Act shall be conclusive for all purposes, and shall not be questioned in any court of law.

4.—(1) In every Bill presented to His Majesty under the preceding provisions of this Act, the words of enactment shall be as follows, that is to say:—

"Be it enacted by the King's most Excellent Majesty, by and with the advice and consent of the Commons in this present Parliament assembled, in accordance with the provisions of the Parliament Act, 1911, and by authority of the same, as follows."

(2) Any alteration of a Bill necessary to give effect to this section shall not be deemed to be an amendment of the Bill. . . .

7. Five years shall be substituted for seven years as the time fixed for the maximum duration of Parliament under the Septennial Act, 1715. . . .

— Reading No. 20 —

THE DEFENSE OF THE REALM CONSOLIDATION ACT, 1914[20]

It is generally agreed that, in times of emergency, governments need unusual powers. In a series of acts

[20] *Public General Statutes,* LIII, 21-22: 5 George V, c. 8.

passed in 1914, which were combined in the Defense of the Realm Consolidation Act of 1914, parliament delegated immense powers to the king in council, actually to the government of the day, for securing the public safety and the defense of the realm. Pertinent excerpts from the Act of 1914, which at the time marked a new high in executive power, are given below. Subsequently, following the war, parliament made standing provision for emergencies that might occur in peacetime by passing an Emergency Powers Act in 1920.

⁂

Be it enacted . . . as follows:

1.—(1) His Majesty in Council has power during the continuance of the present war to issue regulations for securing the public safety and the defense of the realm, and as to the powers and duties for that purpose of the Admiralty and Army Council and of the members of His Majesty's forces and other persons acting in his behalf; and may by such regulations authorise the trial by courts-martial, or in the case of minor offences by courts of summary jurisdiction, and punishment of persons committing offences against the regulations and in particular against any of the provisions of such regulations designed—

(a) to prevent persons communicating with the enemy or obtaining information for that purpose or any purpose calculated to jeopardise the success of the operations of any of His Majesty's forces or the forces of his allies or to assist the enemy; or

(b) to secure the safety of His Majesty's forces and ships and the safety of any means of communication and of railways, ports, and harbours; or

(c) to prevent the spread of false reports or reports likely to cause disaffection to His Majesty or to interfere with the success of His Majesty's forces by land or sea or to prejudice His Majesty's relations with foreign powers; or

(d) to secure the navigation of vessels in accordance

with directions given by or under the authority of the Admiralty; or

(e) otherwise to prevent assistance being given to the enemy or the successful prosecution of the war being endangered.

(2) Any such regulations may provide for the suspension of any restrictions on the acquisition or user of land, or the exercise of the power of making bye-laws, or any other power under the Defense Acts, 1842 to 1875, or the Military Land Acts, 1891 to 1903, and any such regulations or any orders made thereunder. . . .

(3) It shall be lawful for the Admiralty or Army Council—

(a) to require that there shall be placed at their disposal the whole or any part of the output of any factory or workshop in which arms, ammunition, or warlike stores or equipment, or any articles required for the production thereof, are manufactured;

(b) to take possession of and use for the purpose of His Majesty's naval or military service any such factory or workshop or any plant thereof; . . . .

— Reading No. 21 —

THE WAR CABINET REPORT, 1917[21]

All writers on the British constitution before the First World War commented on the secrecy of cabinet proceedings. One of the most striking evidences of the abandonment of complete secrecy by the Lloyd George

[21] *Parliamentary Papers,* 1918, XIV, Cmd. 9005.